PEOPLE WATCHING

by

Neil Taylor

A MISTRAL Publishing Limited Publication.

First published in Great Britain
by Mistral Publishing Ltd. 1991.

Copyright © by Neil Taylor/Mistral Publishing Ltd.

People Watching was written and compiled by Neil Taylor.

A CIP catalogue record for this book is available from the
British Library.

ISBN 1874053006

Front Cover illustration: Julie Marks

Cartoons by David Banks

Typeset by TIL Ltd, 3 Heddon Street, London W1R 7LE.
071 434 1281.

Printed and bound in Great Britain by Waterside Press,
Hatfield, Hertfordshire.

PEOPLE WATCHING

101 Observations

Based on the original idea by Neil Taylor
and dedicated to Oll.

Produced in association with Susan Lister
and Mistral Publishing Ltd.

CONTENTS

INTRODUCTION

There aren't many things you can do in life any more without either

a.)   it costing you plenty of money

b.)   you getting arrested, or

c.)   you dying from it.

People-watching is something you can do any time, any place, anywhere (cue the Martini joke). It's a matter of being aware of what's around you and, once you start, you can't stop and you find you improve at it as time passes. Size is not important and neither is shape. You can be tall, short, fat, thin, loud, soft, thick, brainy – it doesn't matter. So it's better than sex.

People-watching is not subject to VAT. One pays no tax on it. It is not subject to APR 22.8%. Written credit details are not required. You do not have to be a member of FIMBRA or LAUTRO. You don't even have to have stone-cladding on your house.

People-watching is simply what the phrase says, watching people. At home. At work. In a pub. In a restaurant. In the bath. In the garden. In the supermarket, wherever all you have to do is NOTICE what goes on around you. Take time to see what people do in a given situation. How do they react? What do they say? Do they squirm with embarrassment? Or are they squirming because they want to go to the loo?

People are all around us. Some close. Some distant. They're truly funny. We're like sheep. We all copy each other because it makes us more secure. We all have our funny little ways. Just open your eyes and look around. Step back from daily events and take time to observe.

That's people-watching. Use this book to observe typical situations. Take the written exams. Get the degree and then be very aware that, at this moment, there's probably someone watching you looking very thoughtful...

Here we go, then...

ABOUT THE AUTHOR

He's a radio disc jockey. Neil Taylor was born in Rochford, Essex – at the age of 0, like most people. His parents emigrated to Kent in 1960, which is where he lives and works today. After leaving school in 1976 – Chatham House, Ramsgate (Ted Heath's old school) – he worked for a year for the Ministry of Defence. We'd like to tell you more about that era but we can't or we'd have to shoot you due to the Official Secrets Act. Suffice to say that no official records of him exist at this time, probably because they've erased them, which is just as well.

Neil started in radio in 1980 working freelance for national and local stations across the U.K. In 1984 he joined Invicta Radio and eventually hosted the popular evening show. A book about Problem Pages for men was almost penned at that time which probably you would have liked but it was serialised in local papers instead. In 1988 Neil moved to the breakfast show on Invicta, which he's still doing today. He's also Programme Controller at the station, which means he's the one at whom everyone moans when things go wrong.

On a serious note he's had a highly successful career; British Radio awards in 1986, 1987, 1988 and 1990 for different programmes have been eclipsed only by even better performances in the Worldwide Radio awards. In those annual awards, sought after by thousands of radio stations from 28 countries, Neil picked up a Bronze Medal in 1989. In 1990 he won the Gold Medal for Best Radio Personality and a Silver Medal for a special programme. In 1991 he took the top award – the Grand Award – as well as a Gold and two Bronze Medals.

Two 7in. singles, an LP, all kinds of projects, World Records – they've all been tackled. It all sounds a little sickly really but unless you write this kind of stuff about authors, people get upset because they want to know. Don't worry, you haven't wasted your money – the book gets better. He's a fine lad – quiet, shy, introverted, and fun to be with. We'll take the money now. Oh, and he's absolutely crazy about ski-ing and flying. But this week he thought he'd write a book.

THE UNDERWEAR DEPARTMENT OF A LADIES SHOP

This first one is really for men. It's a Saturday morning and you're being dragged to the shops again when you'd really rather by ANYWHERE else. Into the car... the hassle of finding a car parking space... no change in the pocket for the meter and so on. Feelings are already running a little high. You wander in and out of shops in the High Street getting a few necessaries and plenty of unnecessaries when you spy the horror or horrors, the ladies clothes shop. Dorothy Perkins, Laura Ashley, Marks & Spencer – it doesn't matter, they're all the same.

Your partner drags you in, with you screaming at the top of your voice. Not exactly; one knows it's in one's interest to go quietly or one pays for it later. After half an hour your partner finds two or three outfits she likes and she'd like to try them on. So off you both go to the back of the shop where the fitting rooms are.

In she goes and you're left to wait but what's around you at the back of the shop? Knickers, knickers and more knickers. Suspender belts, teddies, stockings and knickers. You can't sit down because there's no chair. You can't look at them because invariably someone will catch you and look at you as if you're some kind of pervert. Flashing a wedding ring does no good because they think you have a mistress. You can't move away or you won't see your partner when she emerges for your vote of approval. So you blush, get very hot and try not to be noticed. Which makes you more noticeable. It's agony and it happens everywhere.

Throughout this book there are some situations for men, some for women and some for asexual, whoever they are. They work equally well for observing both sexes. The foregoing could be you in that situation but, equally well, you could be watching someone else. Try not to laugh when their embarrassment becomes too obvious.

HORRORSCOPES

Why does everyone rely on them so much? There's a wealth of material here. You see people in offices, at home, in pubs, in sports halls – everywhere – all saying the same thing. 'Ooh, are those the horrorscopes – let me see mine.'

They then proceed to take in, word for word, what some old biddy chooses to write that day. Normally they're so general that they could apply to 95% of the human race. Most, not all by any means, are made up by whoever on the newspaper pulls the short straw. It's a difficult job making up 12 horrorscopes day after day or week after week which are different, but made up they are to satisfy the craving we all have for someone to predict good fortune for us that day. Some people have the talent to do it properly and I firmly believe it's possible to do so, but most are made up.

I have had the job of writing horrorscopes for newspapers under another name and I've had people write to me to tell me how accurate my predictions are.

So observe. Watch how people, lemming-like, go for the stars pages in newspapers, magazines and booklets. Watch how their self-esteem soars if the stars say something good. Watch how mentally they make a note to change things if the stars are not so good. In short, watch how SOME people plan their lives around the stars.

THE SINGLE EYEBROW

There can't be many things more disconcerting than meeting someone face to face who has a single eyebrow. The kind of eyebrow which leaps out at you when you look. The kind of eyebrow which says 'Look, I'm an eyebrow. Mow me'.

Normally the owner of said eyebrow is completely unaware that it is a problem. No-one has ever had the courage to tell them. The left eyebrow makes a pass at the right eyebrow at some point in the unfortunate owner's life and an attempt at physical union is made. As it happens over a period of time the brow's escapades go largely unnoticed until one day they've joined and let no man put asunder what God has joined together. As if they could.

Cut them back and they grow twice as fast. Pluck them and you keep knocking your head on the bath when you faint from the pain. It also leaves unsightly holes in your face when you pull out the stems and roots of an eyebrow.

A single eyebrow is one of those afflictions with which it is impossible to dispense, unless you resort to terror tactics like blowlamps, weedkiller and the like.

So observe at your leisure the single eyebrow and ask the owner for an autograph, because perfectly-formed ones are very rare.

HAIR

Have you ever realised that hair is dead? It is. It's all dead cells mashed together. They only live bit is the root in your head. The rest of it is very dead. Which makes it all the more strange that we all spend so much time playing with it. After all, if a rabbit, tortoise, cat, dog or fish of ours were suddenly to expire, you wouldn't bleach it, would you? Or dry it with a dryer? Or perm it? Or colour it? Or wash it every other day?

We do this to our hair because we're humans and we're very odd creatures. Consequently, we all walk around with dead stuff on the top of our heads arranged in a variety of patterns and styles because it looks good.

Some, however, do it more than others. Observe if you will the person who goes into the office weekly with different colour hair. What is the first thing we say to someone who's had their hair cut? Eh? Usually, it's something along the lines of 'Hello, have you had a haircut?' 'Yes, I have actually – do you like it?' 'Yes, I think it suits you. It makes you look much younger'.

Always said with sincerity but do you go through the same rigmarole when you spot someone has cut their nails?

Consider this exchange...

'Your hair looks nice, have you washed it?'

'Yes, I have. Thank you'.

Do you ever approach someone and comment on the fact that they've washed their hands? Or their feet? Or their bottom?

Observe then the weird and wonderful things people do with their hair. The things we all say and then ask yourself why we all do it.

OVERHEARING RESTAURANT CONVERSATION

The restaurant is probably one of the best places for people watching as, generally, they are places where people are socially at their easiest. A number of situations occur in this book based on restaurant behaviour and you could do no worse than put yourself in an eating house for a night and just look all around you.

Overhearing conversation is a good one for PW novices as it's so easy to spot. Wherever you sit in a restaurant, you'll see and hear people talking louder and louder as they drink more and more. At some point you'll easily be able to spot people on the closest tables trying to hear what they're saying. It's like the 'crossed line syndrome'. If you have a crossed line on the phone you're supposed to put it down immediately. Do you? Do you hell. You hang on and listen to what they're saying. We all do it because we're basically nosy.

Because your inhibitions fall in a restaurant in proportion to the amount you drink it's easier for people to overhear conversations later in the evening. Thus it's easier to spot people doing it and it all becomes very embarrassing if the people talking catch someone listening in. It's also very rude to do this but when did that ever prevent it?

THE OFFICE PEN STEALER/HOARDER

There are deeper meanings to this whole scenario. What kind of person becomes a secretive pen stealer? Why do they do it? What do they do with all the pens? Were they abused as children?

Try this as your first practical bit of people watching. Take any old pen, a BIC biro will do, and place it on any desk in an open office. Go for a cup of coffee and gossip. On your return the pen will have gone. Unless you are stinking rich and can afford to have a homing device fitted to all your pens you now have a problem. Your pen has been stolen and you haven't an earthly chance of finding it.

You now scan your list of options. Do you:

(i)   Burst into tears and have a breakdown?

(ii)   Call the police?

(iii) Write to your MP?

(iv)   Resign?

None of that gets back your pen, so you might as well track down the thief. For what clues are you looking? What kind of person would borrow and not return your pen? Are they furtive? Do they have a beard or a moustache?

Look for a place to which secret hoards of pens migrate and breed, generally in the southern/warmer parts of an office. Pen breeding occurs twice yearly in the spring and autumn, so keep your wits about you at those times. If you strike lucky and your PW skills are honed to a razor's edge, you'll catch the villain. Point out the error of their ways forcefully and make them promise not to do it again.

COUPLES WHO ARE BORED WITH EACH OTHER

Love is a well-chronicled subject. Two hearts meet; they are mutually attracted; they go out for the evening; one asks the other in for coffee – not really meaning coffee and so on. After much bonking and passage of time the mutual attraction sometimes dims. The sight of the same pert rear in too small underpants becomes boring. More pert rears are craved; but because we're all decent people at heart, sometimes we stay with that person because we think we're being kind. We don't want to hurt the other person's feelings.

This is a very decent, British, honourable thing to do but when you're out socially it shows you're bored. However much you try, the boredom shines through. It happens with young couples, old couples, couples with and without children, even couples with hamsters. It happens with married couples and couples living in a large measure of sin.

Next time you're out, spot the bored couple. It's the couple opposite each other in a pub saying nothing – just sitting there with half a drink on the table. Occasionally, she will look around at other people. He will scratch his ears. They will look so bored.

Or in a restaurant. It is the couple on a table for two. No hand-holding here. No footsie under the table. No visual undressing going on. Nope. Just plain conversation like 'Vegetables are nice, aren't they?' or 'The lampshades are quaint, aren't they?' punctuated by long bursts of silence. There may be a near riot all round them wherever they are but they are oblivious to it. They're just bored. In a minute they'll get up, walk out to the car, go home, have a Horlicks, and go to bed. Each will follow precisely the same actions and events they always do, at the same time every day. They are the bored couple but it leads us nicely to...

THE CREATURE OF HABIT

This is the individual who does everything the same day, at the same time, no matter what. They can be spotted anywhere. They get up every morning at exactly the same time. They get out of the same side of the bed. They walk exactly the same number of steps to the bathroom. They turn on the shower to exactly the same setting as yesterday, regardless of outside temperature. They count the brush strokes while brushing their teeth and never deviate. Then they go to the loo.

They have the same breakfast – 'You'd never catch me going without my cereal, John'. They walk the dog the same route ... they kiss their partner goodbye in precisely the same way as usual and they go to work.

They follow the same route daily, passing the same marker points at exactly the same time. They enter their workplace through the same door and put their hat and coat on the same peg. They sit in the same seat, at the same desk, facing the same window. At 11.05 they have one cup of coffee from the drinks machine, two halves of sandwich wrapped in silver foil and a banana. Then they go to the loo.

They always answer the phone in the same way; they position everything on their desk the same and they sit the same.

At lunchtime they eat the same rotation of meals every week. Pork on Monday. Fish on Tuesday. Mince on Wednesday. Lamb on Thursday and Pizza on Friday 'cos it's the weekend. They spend exactly the same amount of time eating, no matter what food it is. Then they go to the loo.

Yippee. It's time to go home and off they go. Same route, same markers, same faces, same statements – everything the same.

In the evening they watch the same programmes on the TV on the same days each week. They have a cup of tea at 7.58 when the advertisements are on. They walk the dog the same route as in the morning. They do the washing up and leave everything in exactly the same place as ever, ready for the morning. Then they go to the bathroom, brush their teeth, wash and go to bed having sex once a week on Sunday mornings. Then they go to the loo.

Pretty boring, eh? There's probably one near you now.

WINE GLASS ON THE TABLE – PRACTICAL EXPERIMENT

How can you tell if someone fancies you, even if they're not supposed to? You could ask them but it might not get you very far. Anyway, out of modesty, they might not tell you.

So how can you tell if someone, married or single, available or unavailable, really fancies you? You could try playing footsie when you're out eating – but that is dangerous. You could end up playing with the wrong person – perhaps of the same sex or perhaps even your partner – by mistake. You could even end up getting a smack in the teeth from someone.

No. What is needed is a foolproof, subliminal way of discovering 100% if they're locked on to you. So here's something you could try which works. When you're next in a restaurant, your wine glass is usually at the top right-hand side of your place setting, unless you're some type of oddball. When you drink from your glass – sitting opposite the person you suspect is visually undressing you – put down your glass next to theirs but without touching it. This is difficult to do because it means you have to put it down some way away from its usual position. In fact, it's normally forward to the top left-hand side position. When they next drink from theirs, that is the key. If they put it down in a position close to your glass, you're in. If they put it away from your glass equally out of position you're out of luck. If they put the glass down next to yours and it actually touches, making a noise, you are so in you might as well get under the table.

How and why this works is simple. We all love our own portion of territory. By putting your glass out of position, you're 'invading' their territory. So when they next drink, it's what they do about it that counts. By putting it back next to yours they are 'inviting' you into their territory and, in fact, welcoming it. By moving their glass away they are recreating their own territory of which they do not want you to be a part. Of course, if your advances are rejected you don't get embarrassed.

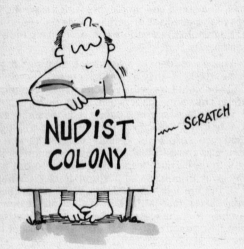

AN ITCH IN AN EMBARRASSING PLACE

The surface area of our bodies is some massive amount, if you were to lay out all the skin flat. One doesn't do that often or all your bones would fall out. On that massive surface area live trillions of microscopic bugs with many legs and big teeth. Their whole purpose in life is to munch their way through as much of you as they can before they fall off and die. It is not a pleasant existence but they didn't choose it.

Little wonder, then, that from time to time we itch. Sometimes the itching is due to some form of pox or virus which brings you out in lumps, bumps and spots. Those, for the purposes of this scenario, we can discard. We're talking about the kind of itch which is inflicted by thousands of the little blighters munching in unison, usually in the region 99% of the population doesn't see.

We've all had that feeling; a battalion of bugs synchronise their munching around your private parts and you have a terrible urge to scratch there and annihilate them *en masse*. You can't, because if you did people would think you were playing with yourself. So we've all devised very clever ways of being able to disguise the fact that we are scrunching our privates to alleviate the itch without being noticed. Most times it works but sometimes it fails dismally.

Astute PW persons beware. La intimate scratching is fairly easy to spot if you keep your eyes open and the 'rewards' are usually one very embarrassed person when they find you gawping at them. Juvenile – yes. Satisfying – particularly. Especially if it's your boss.

MEN IN SHOWERS

This is one for the men, although women will doubtless find it amusing. It may even happen in female showers. I don't know; I've never had the good fortune to be in one. You have to be very careful here or people may well get the wrong idea. If you are caught looking at someone of the same sex in a shower, you are liable to a.) get your teeth smashed in or b.) find someone smiling at you. Both may be equally unpalatable, so be careful.

It is a proven fact that men worry about the size of their equipment. 'Size is not important', scream the women's magazines. Well, they would – they haven't got one to worry about. It may be a surprise to some women but men DO worry, no matter how much they are reassured.

So, in a situation when there are other exposed males around, it is only natural that, very discreetly, comparisons are made. That can either put you in a really good mood or an incredibly bad one, depending on how nature designed you.

In the showers after any kind of sport is the place where it usually happens. You're happily taking a shower when in walks another man. Immediately, most men discreetly turn their backs but, equally discreetly, most men, if they're honest, will try and get a passing look. The trouble is that men aren't honest and would never admit it. Equally troublesome is that size is affected by temperature and thus false 'readings' can be given.

It's a grey area for people watching but it's not crude or even rude. It's nature and one usually finds that those who laugh and joke the loudest to keep up their self-confidence usually have little to shout about. Sadly, most women will never know.

Does the same situation happen with women? I wouldn't know.

SHAVING – AND THOSE MISSED SPOTS

There are plenty of PW scenarios which involve noticing something about someone else and then not having the courage to say anything. Shaving is one of those. Part of the daily chore – where no matter how carefully you mow yourself it's back next day looking as bad as ever. Fashion pundits have tried to make 'designer stubble' stick but to achieve a scruffy look you have to trim it anyhow or you end up looking ridiculous.

Most people never have time to shave properly. Bathrooms are notoriously over-populated places in the average household and even booking space doesn't seem to work. Then there's the electric-blade argument. There can't be many a shaver who hasn't slashed himself to pieces because of bumps, spots, being jogged, and so on – but it does shave you close, even if it takes off half your skin. So the alternative is the electric razor.

That has the advantage of being reasonably quick if not so accurate. That brings in this scenario. A quick flick over with the electric razor suffices for most of us each day but you always miss certain parts and it looks stupid when it's pointed out to you. Little tufts of stubble sticking out under your chin can be noticeable by 5 o'clock in the evening and there's not much you can do about it. The office guillotine is a little impracticable.

It's not just men, either. When you look through the book, there's an equally applicable one for women. Perhaps if you notice this on someone the kindest thing might be to ignore it.

SLEEPING POSITIONS

Researchers and scientists will tell you that how we sleep affects how we are. Do you sleep deeply or do you just doze very lightly? Do you need a good deal of sleep or just a few hours?

Each of us is different and one fact not often researched about sleep is the different positions in which people sleep. We might face many a crisis during our waking hours but, when it comes to sleeping, we each return to our 'natural' position where we feel most comfortable.

If you're really tired, invariably you can fall asleep in any position. If you're going to bed normally, you tend to have to adopt the same position before you call fall asleep. It's a little like breathing and swallowing; you do both naturally all the time but the minute you become conscious of it, you start to notice it and vary it.

So what are you? Do you lie on your back? Or your side? Or your front? Back sleepers are supposed to be more 'macho' than other types; front sleepers are supposed to need more loving and caring. Why, I haven't a clue but it brings out some good people watching.

Try and spot the front sleepers. It would certainly make a good chat-up line in the pub. 'Excuse me, but I wonder if I might ask you – do you sleep on your back or your front?'

Front sleepers by definition would be shyer, more quiet types than back sleepers, who would tend to be more dominant, aggressive, and loud. There are, however, variations to every rule; do your own survey.

WHEN SOMEONE FANCIES YOU – PART 2

The wine glass experiment in number 9 may give you a firm indication that someone really has the hots for you. There is another way which shows whether someone really likes you or not, althought it has its limitations.

Some parts of our bodies we can control, some we can't; try telling that to a judge. The eyes are a great giveaway as they are uncontrollable. They give away so many secrets.

For instance, when you're bored and you're in conversation with someone, you cannot hold their gaze for any time. Your eyes will betray you automatically by flicking away constantly as if they are distracted. A person who is watching you reasonably closely would pick this up. Likewise, if you're lying about something your eyes will give you away.

If you have a fancy for someone the eyes are the great betrayers. Your body undergoes a series of emotions and reflexes but the most obvious one is that the pupils – the dark bits – in your eyes dilate; i.e., they get bigger than normal.

The PW aspect is easy to spot but you have to be careful; if you're in dim or subdued lighting the pupils dilate naturally to let in more light. Also, if the person is tired, again they will dilate. So, with a tired person in a dimly-lit room, their eyes will tell you nothing – but it works, albeit in limited fashion.

SHELLSUITS

Described universally as the worst fashion garment of the 90s, the shellsuit picks up where the ubiquitous two-piece towelly leisure suit left off. When aerobics caught on in the early 80s, the industry had to have a certain style of garment everyone could buy and thus feel a part of the 'set'. This would generate more money – and it did. Leotards were tried but some whale-shaped 22-stoners didn't really look right with bits of them squeezed into outfits two sizes too small. So the two-piece towelly, stretchy, outfits were introduced from size 8 to size 28 and horrific they looked, too. Everyone was rounded off to two sizes too big and derrieres hung from those things as if there was a harpoon aimed at them. They sold for a time but people eventually realised that, despite looking trendy, they looked particularly gross and ugly.

Unperturbed, the fashion industry was working on a follow-up. A garment was needed which made the person look athletic, was thin so as not to accentuate the flab, hung loosely enough for the same reason and looked expensive enough to justify a £100 tag. So the shellsuit was born.

Again, like lemmings, people rushed out and parted with their hard-earned cash to get one. All shapes, all sizes, all with sponsors' logos and makes; they were, and still are, everywhere. This time round they look better but you can still find some horrific examples if you look hard enough. Keep your eyes open in supermarkets, leisure clubs, pubs and sports grounds and you'll see some sights.

SWIMMING COSTUMES

This is a PW for a day when you're really bored at work, as it requires plenty of daydreaming and imagination. As you look around you at your colleagues, what do you see? Posy people, stuffy people, prim people, outrageous, sexy, tarty, smart, scruffy and old/young people. All have their own identities you can recognise easily.

So what would they look like on the beach on holiday? A little visual undressing never hurt anyone and you can probably imagine where all the requisite lumps and bumps would show – but what kind of swimming costume would they choose to wear?

Would Miss 'prim and proper' wear a stunningly low-cut, slashed to the waistband, one-piece outfit? Would Mr Poser wear the most old-fashioned 'far-too-tight' swimming trunks which looked as if they were crippling him? Would people who look sexy at work necessarily have the courage to unwrap themselves on holiday?

Is there a correlation between the kind of swimming costume a person chooses and their personality? For example, do solicitors wear trunks with spots? Do showbiz types wear luminous outfits? Do Marks & Spencer sales assistants wear 1950s style cover-up jobbies?

You'd probably be very surprised if you ever saw them on holiday – and the chances are you won't. Why do you think people go to so much trouble to hide 'swimming costume style' snapshots from their holiday photos when they return home?

Try it at work and see how accurate you are. Promiscuous adults do this PW regularly but with underwear instead of swimming outfits but that's far too rude for this book. Strange, though, because essentially they are the same types of clothing. One is considered 'rude' and personal, the other isn't.

GLAMOUR MODELS' (see Front Cover)

These you can spot anywhere. Everyone but everyone knows one. Not, I hasten to add, fully-professional models who earn a fortune doing 101 poses in very expensive clothes for magazines but people who THINK they have it in them to become glamour models. They are invariably female. They have high-pitched, whiny voices. They are hopeless at getting up in the morning. They have many moods – and that's just the start.

Their mum does their hair, once a week. Usually a 'natural' blonde, they take the somewhat unusual step of having their roots died black to achieve that subtle two-tone look. Their most valuable possession is a curly brush, followed by curling tongs, followed by four hair dryers with 53 attachments. They agonise over getting the curls just right in their hair so that they can swish it from side to side in public.

Then come the clothes. Tight. Short. Noticeable – and gaudy. Easy. Next, the accessories, always carried about in a large Ibiza-style carrier bag. Mirror. Hairbrush. Perfume x 3 – (usually Beautiful, Poison or similar). Lipstick. Nail varnish. Nail varnish remover so that said Glamour Model can pick it off on the train to work and 'do' 'er nails' again in front of everyone. Spare tights. Wrinkle cream. Moisturiser. Make-up of all kinds. *Cosmopolitan* magazine. Nail file. Tweezers for eyelashes. Spare knickers, in case the originals are forgotten after a modelling session; and so on.

Finally, where do you watch for them? Potential Glamour Models work behind the counter in banks, chemists or department stores, the latter two in the beauty departments to be exact. You can't miss them. The biggest give-away is when they speak. They are 'airheads'. Thick. No brains – but glamorous; and always ready for the 'shoot'.

THE RESTAURANT WAITRESS

This follows on well from our Glamour Models. Because they have the same tendencies. Here we are talking Harvesters restaurants, Beefeaters, Berni Inns, Little Chefs — you name it, you'll find 'em. You're out for the evening with friends and you fancy a meal. Ah, a Harvester. Perfect. Pull in, park the car, and in you go...

'We'd like a table for four, please'.

'Certainly Sir. Have you ever eaten at a Harvester before?'

'Er, no. We haven't'.

'Well, I'm an airhead with no brains and I've just finished my training course. You'll find the experience of eating here unlike any other. All our food is freshly cooked by Martin our chef... (two minute ramble)... would you like to sit here, please, thank you. My name is Karen and I'll be your waitress this evening. If there's anything you require just call me and I'll fix my plastic grin for you and come running. Would you like a bread roll?'

'Er, no, but we'd like a drink please'.

'Certainly sir. What would you like?' (Big toothy smile here).

Drinks are duly ordered and arrive.

'Here are your menus. The chef's special is rubber steak coated with marinated loo roll. It's very nice — I can thoroughly recommend it (giggle). Are you ready to order?'

'We've only just got the menus. Can you give us a few minutes to choose?'

'Certainly, sir. Are you ready to order now? Would you like a fresh home-baked roll?' (continues till batteries run out).

If you think this is a little harsh and that everyone has to do something for a living, I **suppose** you're correct but try noticing this next time you're in a place like this. Now you've read this, I guarantee you won't be able to prevent a smile crossing your face at some point. You've usually had enough by the time you get the mega plastic smile and the 'Enjoy your meal' platitude.

VIDEO CAMERAS

One of life's great recent inventions. Ten years ago they were unknown. Now, they bring out the best and worst in people. Twenty years ago the worst you had to face when you came of age was 'the photo album'. Your parents would wait until you'd found a really attractive partner for whom you'd die and out would come 'the photo album' of your history since birth over the Sunday tea table.

'This was Susan when she was two...' and there's a picture of you in your Sunday best dribbling all over everyone. 'And this is a picture of David when he was six...' as the picture reveals a toothless grinning David peeing in the sink.

Nowadays, video cameras capture the full horror of it all. At 17 years of age the same nervous Susan or David, family and new partner sit at the Sunday tea table. 'I know,' says the mother. 'Let's show your new partner the video of you being born' – and out it comes. Birth. Toddlerism. Childhood. Nasty accident. Chicken pox. Measles. And all. In far more striking detail than any photos could reveal.

What of the people who own video cameras? Some people compile sensible video collections of interesting things such as holidays, family occasions and the like. Though when they get time to sit down and watch them all goodness only knows. Others just go berserk. Stick a camcorder in their hands and they'll video ANYTHING. A tree. A bush. A lampost. A dog. A bus. The lawn. The front door. The bathroom. Aunt Edith sunbathing topless. Literally, anything. Can you imagine being invited to the house of those people and having to watch a compilation of horrors like this? 'George has a new video camera you know. Would you like to see some of his work?' (Never say yes).

This really is where the PW aspect comes in. Next time you see someone with a video camera, take time to watch what it is that they are filming. Few people have the facilities to edit their masterpieces, so imagine what the poor viewers have to sit through. When you start watching for this you'll be mortified at the inane things people film.

CONFRONTING PEOPLE WHO'VE BEEN GOSSIPING ABOUT YOU

It's probably fair to say that we all hate being talked about. None of us is that secure that we can't be affected by other people saying things behind our backs – and it happens all the time. You could be the most popular person in the world and people would STILL find things to talk about behind your back.

Most of the time we don't know about it but, sometimes, someone lets it slip that so-and-so said such and such about you – and you see red. After some super-sleuth detective work you manage to cobble together some 'proof' and off you go for the kill.

This is a particularly good example of People Watching if you can master sufficient self-control to be able to step back from the heat of the moment and watch the other person.

Let's take a specific example. One of the people in your office at work has been saying that you're a tart. You'll go off with anybody. Your nickname is Martini. In fact, you're a Vestal virgin. After you've come down from the ceiling when someone has let it slip accidentally that people think this about you, you set about confronting the gossiper. You amass 'statements' from friends, 'proof' from other sources, and you collar said gossiper for the showdown.

'Such-and-such says that you've been saying this about me and I have proof. What have you to say about it before I make access to your teeth more difficult for cleaning?'

You wouldn't seek this confrontation unless you were 110% sure of yourself, so you know you're right and they're wrong. The interesting part and the PW aspect is how, even though they know they're in the wrong, they try to wriggle out of it. Watching it is very amusing but you need a great deal of self-control to handle it.

HOW PEOPLE CHANGE WHEN IN UNIFORM

At school, we're made to wear uniforms to make us all 'uniform'; it's as simple as that. One pupil can't make another feel bad because they come from a rich enough background to afford nice clothes whereas another can't. It seems to work and by the time we're all unleashed into the big, wide world we're accustomed to wearing a uniform of sorts. Why is it then, when people settle into their chosen professions, that they undergo a total change of character whenever they put on a uniform?

Policemen and women at home or in the pub are presumably normal, reasonable people. Are they the same in their uniform with a blue light on their head? Army, Navy or RAF types – are they the same without their work outfits?

Often referred to as 'Jobsworths', menial posts are often staffed by people who turn into 'mini Hitlers' once they've donned their work uniform. Car park attendants, security guards of all types, traffic wardens, lollypop women, shop assistants – you name it, we've all met one at some time or other.

"You can't park here, sir."

"Why not?"

"Because I said so and I'm in charge. I've got a uniform. You haven't. You're a peasant. So push off."

All very reasonable stuff and, for some reason, none of us will answer back someone who is 'in uniform', even though we're probably right to do so. A uniform seems to shout 'status' at us and we're made to feel subservient. Watch for yourself.

SPOTTING A MAN WHO'S HAD COSMETIC SURGERY

The 1980s were, if you believe all the women's magazines, a boom time for women reshaping themselves to improve their looks. Pages and pages of magazines were littered with tales of the famous having their breasts enlarged or reduced, hips shaven, tummy bulges removed, bum reshapen, and so on. With some it's obviously worked; others have had spectacular failures.

Now for the 90s, it would appear to be the turn of men to get in on the act. It's now reported that there are more men than women in the world, so it follows that men will have to try harder to look better in order to attract a mate. Obviously some things can be worked on fairly easily, like beer bellies, flabbiness in general, sloth-like appearances and so on but a new range of cosmetic surgery is now available for the man who wants to change his image once and for all. Here's a list of some of the things on offer at current prices:

Hair. Can be sewn on to bald patches. Bald bits can be reduced by surgery. Scalps can be remodelled. £2,000+

Eyes. Bags and crows feet can be removed. £1,000+

Ears. Dumbo jobs can be pinned back. £1,100+

Nose. Concorde, flares and hump jobs can be chopped. £2,200+

Chin. Double chins can be removed by liposuction. £1,200+

Chest. Silicone implants to make you look like Schwarzenegger. Silly if you have wimpy limbs, though. £2,200+.

Stomach. Liposuction is the lazy man's way to removing a beer belly. £2,200+.

Bum. A reduction and uplift. £3,000+

The only thing which cannot have its shape and size altered is **that** thing. Because its size changes to suit a variety of situations one cannot make a multi-sized implant.

Presumably, if men are to have all this drastic stuff done to them in the 90's, it will show in some shape or form. Look for lines, large sums on credit card statements, sudden boosts in confidence, loads of new clothes and pleased-looking partners. People for whom it hasn't worked will be easier to spot.

TOOTHPICKS

What a strange invention and custom a toothpick is. We're back in restaurants again. On the table, when you are having a meal, rests the usual complement of gadgets. Plates. Cutlery. Glasses. Plastic flower. Salt, pepper and mustard. Table number. Serviettes. Ashtray. And toothpicks.

Toothpicks are there for your convenience. After all, you wouldn't want to depart from the restaurant heading for a night of unbridled lust with half a cow stuck between your teeth, would you? So the restaurant thoughtfully provides a gadget for you to prise out the cow from between your molars. Some toothpicks are wooden, which have their disadvantages – they usually break and then take up residence with aforementioned cow between your teeth. Others are plastic and they bend at the vital moment but what an odd thing to put on a dinner table anyway?

Why do restaurants not provide those cotton-tipped bud things so that you can pick/clean your ears or nose before you leave? Equally important, one would have thought, to have ones orifices clean? Or why not syringes for the convenience of diabetics? A hairbrush perhaps to make sure that your hair is OK? Or a mirror just to check that the make-up is OK? Surely the place for toothpicks is in the cloakrooms — (restroom if you're American, Honey.)

Toothpicks, however, are at present on the dinner table and in any restaurant, at any time, you can see the most delightful sights of people undertaking corrective surgery on their teeth with a mini spear while you're still eating. It's delightful. It's fascinating. It's People Watching.

DRESS SENSE

We've all, at some stage, been victims of fashion. Nobody likes to feel that they're out-of-date unless they consciously take the decision to drop out of society. It would probably be pretty frightening to add up how much you spend on clothes throughout your life. Wouldn't perhaps two or three uniform outfits do for every day of the week all year round if you were being basic?

No. We all buy clothes and we all pass them sooner or later to brothers, sisters, family or jumble sales. Each of us is an individual with different interpretations of what looks good on either ourselves or someone else.

Why do some people choose to look utterly ridiculous? Strip away the section of people on whom we always comment, viz. 'you wouldn't catch me dead wearing something like that' and you're left with a certain kind of someone who seems to go out of the way to look utterly stupid.

Usually you can spot them in shopping centres on Saturday afternoons. Reds, yellows, pinks, greens, blues, mauves — all mixed together and that's just the hair. Then come the clothes. Hideous. The whole effect is usually rounded off by size 12 Doc Martens' boots finished in deepest noir black. It's not necessarily confined to teenagers, which is probably what you're visualising now; some people seem to have made an art form out of looking like something from outer space. The funny thing is they don't seem at all self-conscious of what they're wearing or the fact that everyone is gawping at them and laughing behind their backs.

PEOPLE WHO KEEP ON SUNGLASSES
INSIDE A BUILDING

By now, you're probably beginning to see for yourself how People Watching works and how it breaks down into types of people, areas of life, places and so on. The one section good for PW above any other is the poser set.

Another great invention, sunglasses were devised so that we don't all go around squinting in the bright sunlight. A useful gadget surely. Did King Harold have a pair of Raybans in the Battle of Hastings? No, because if he had he wouldn't have got an arrow in the eye. Did Henry the Eighth pose in a pair of Wayfarers when watching the Mary Rose sink? Can't recall it. Napoleon might have been armless enough but did you ever see a picture of him wearing Porsche Carrera shades? Neither did I.

So in the late 20th century we've become wimps. They did without shades; we can't. We'll have to accept that. When the sun is out you can spot 1,001 versions of sunglasses from the cheapo to the mega-expensive. And let's be honest, they look good on most people, don't they?

Why do certain people insist on keeping them on when they go inside a building from being out in the sun? Not only do you continually find them walking into cupboards, doors, walls and other people but they look so remarkably silly. There's no discrimination between the sexes. Women and men can be found standing or sitting posing indoors in sunglasses. When you point out to them tactfully that there isn't much sun in the accounts department they generally look at you as if you're insane. Then they simply put them back on again.

One wonders about their nocturnal habits. Presumably they all wear snorkels in bed.

FAKE SUNTANS

There are people, still, who earn sufficient money to have a good 'sun' holiday in the middle of winter. They are the ones who are lying on the beach in the Caribbean while you are digging your car out of your drive in the snow. No matter. You're not envious. You're not that kind of person. They work hard. How they spend their money is up to them. You're not even jealous when they return to work on a Monday morning virtually black when you're standing there in your moonboots. You can cope with it; no problem.

With what you do have a problem is the people who seem to have a suntan all year round. When it hasn't been sunny and when you know they haven't had a holiday in months. They are the fake suntanners. Easy to spot, those people are usually orange in colour. They think they look brown but they're decidedly orange. Why they want to have a year-round tan when the rest of us look so pale others think we've escaped from a morgue is battling. The effort they have to put into keeping tanned is extraordinary.

Method 1 is the sunbed. Some reports say that they give you skin cancer, others say they rot the skin long term; but they work and the results are reasonably natural but it's hard work keeping up the regime of lying on the bed day in, day out.

Method 2 is the rub-on stuff. These are the real oranges. They just about look OK in normal weather but when it's very hot, or they get wet, it goes all streaky. Plus they have to smear it on every day. Yuk.

Method 3 is the pill. You're supposed to swallow one every day and, hey presto, out comes a suntan. How this works defies all known science but if it makes you that colour on the outside, what on earth does it do to your insides and what are the side effects?

Perhaps you've never seen someone with a fake suntan. If you haven't, then keep your eyes open. Watch them daily. It's not voyeurism. It's simply amusing.

26

HAY-FEVER SUFFERERS

Possibly one of the most unfortunate sections of society. Nobody has any real sympathy for them. There is no known cure. People usually think they've got a cold and avoid them but you can shake hands with them. You can even cuddle them. Heavens above, you can even kiss them. Nobody really knows how you catch hay-fever. Perhaps it's via syringe needles if you take drugs. Perhaps it's transmitted sexually. Perhaps you can get it from blood transfusions – but for sure, you can't catch it from toilet seats.

Hay-fever has not a great deal to do with hay. The author is a certified hay-fever sufferer who wouldn't recognise a haystack at 10 feet, let alone ever rolled in one. It's simply an allergy to pollen(s). These are 16-legged microscopic creatures with huge – (relatively speaking) – teeth which get up your nose and make you sneeze uncontrollably.

Hay-fever sufferers' misery begins when they wake up. They sneeze uncontrollably. They can scarcely breathe. Their eyes itch so badly that they feel like pulling them out and their throat is dryer than a Mid Kent Water reservoir in a flood. This is because the pollen(s) have laid eggs up the nose overnight.

It continues unabated throughout the day, no matter what the official pollen count is, ends only when the sufferer becomes unconscious through fatigue at night. Then they get woken through the night as the pollen(s) jostle for position in the nostrils.

Tablets, potions, injections and anti-histamines all fail to alleviate any of the symptoms. Hay-fever sufferers just suffer. Badly – and their plight is ignored by the civilised world. AAH! - Action Against Hay-fever is the world body which is co-ordinating the fight against the disease which can affect any of us at any time – usually the summer. An antidote is being sought urgently. Funds are much needed. Pressure is being brought to bear. YOU CAN HELP.

Identify a hay-fever sufferer by the loo roll hanging round their neck. Make them feel wanted. Cuddle them profusely and make them feel that they are not an outcast from society.

HOLIDAY BORES

A holiday, by definition, is a break from your usual surroundings. A chance to relax. A chance to recharge the batteries. We all need one at some time or other. Holidays are also a great occasion for people watching. Observing how people change when they're away, the things they do. Observing someone's almost total change in character. You could write a book on that itself.

What happens when someone returns from holiday? You sometimes feel a little like a fish out of water for the first few days you're back because you're not aware of events, politics and happenings around you. You rush to the shop to have your photos developed. Also, if you're not careful, you can become a holiday bore.

It's always pleasant to see a friend or colleague return from holiday; usually they're full of vigour, they look good, and everyone enjoys their return but that can fade very quickly as they relate stories of the holiday continually...

'Oh, it wasn't like that in Greece. Do you know, when Sandra and I went out one evening...'

'Heh, you say that but Dave and Angela whom we met on holiday said that...'

'You should see how they cope with that in Greece. Did you know that when...'

Ring any bells? It's the first signs of a true holiday bore. A person who has to relate everything back to the holiday. A person who is oblivious to the fact that no-one else has the slightest clue about what they're talking because they weren't there.

Holiday bores can also bore everyone else silly simply by constantly flashing around their photos.

UNDER THE THUMB

Comedians have made jokes about this for years. People who are under the directions and orders of another and do nothing to resist or change it but how do you spot them? It's very easy. A person who is under the thumb will never be able to make a decision for themselves. Ask them out for the evening and they'll always have to seek permission from the other half.

They will always defer to that same other half in all matters that concern them. When shopping it will be their partner who chooses their clothes. Or perfume/aftershave. Or food. Or cosmetics. Their partner will always decide what they're doing that evening. Where they're going on holiday. What major purchase they'll make next.

Their partner will invariably order for them in a restaurant. Dominate the conversation. Humiliate the thumbprintee. And probably tell them when to go to the loo as well.

It all develops fairly early in any relationship as one person tries to dominate the other for reasons of insecurity, upbringing, or plain insensitivity to their partner. Sometimes it can be frighteningly obvious to everyone around them, yet they can't see it themselves. If it's pointed out to them they become very defensive and try to demonstrate how absurdly untrue it all is. The louder they shout and the more they try to convince everyone else that they do not have their thumb on their partner the truer the whole thing is – and the worse it gets.

THE DOCTOR'S SURGERY

A positive wealth of PW here. None of us particularly likes going to the doctor because we usually have some kind of pox or disease when we go there. Mind you, some people use it as a kind of social meeting place and they're the first ones for whom to watch. The regulars... 'Oh hello, Joan. How are you? Have you had a good week?'... 'Oh, yes, the usual. Doctor says I must take it easy, you know'.

Another breed easy to spot in the waiting room are the hypochondriacs. They are the people who ALWAYS have something wrong with them from the minute they wake and they make YOU feel ill just looking at them.

Others to spot are the habitualists. There's always the one who makes a song and dance about getting up and reading through the magazines every five minutes, loudly turning all the pages. Then there's the professional mother showing off her baby to anyone who cares to look and making a great show of constantly arranging and rearranging the poor child's clothes. How about the baby watcher who always coos with delight at any baby in the room... 'Oh, what a lovely baby. Simply gorgeous. You're so lucky to have such a good-looking baby'. Usually the baby in question has a squashed prune-looking face and enough hair on it to attract an ape.

Then there's the proverbial old person who takes 15 minutes to shuffle from the reception desk to a vacant seat, moaning loudly. 'Blinking waiting rooms. They weren't like this when I was young'. The number fiddler. The person who sits holding their number fiddling with it as if they're on death row.

Other things to observe. How everyone jumps when the buzzer goes. How everyone is in awe of 'Doctor'. How some people don't look sick at all. How you're probably sitting next to someone with the most contagious disease known to man. How people always flash their prescription leaflet when they emerge from the doctor as if to say 'See, I told you I was ill. Look, I am. See. I'm ill. Official. Here's my proof. I'm no timewaster'.

Then the most annoying one of all. The howling baby and how no-one attempts to even quieten the thing. It just sits there and howls. There's plenty more; once you've spotted these you'll see for yourself.

THAT EMBARRASSED LOOK

TV shows run on it. Commentators score by it and we all suffer from it. That moment when we've been caught out. We've either done something wrong and been discovered or something has happened and we've been acutely embarrassed.

Each of us reacts in a different way at the moment of truth. TV shows like The Generation Game were founded on this exact theme of the embarrassed look and the camera always focuses in at the point where the contestant feels about one inch big. Conversely, all of us delight in other peoples' embarrassment and it's that which makes TV shows work.

Most common is the blush. It's not something you can control. You're embarrassed and you feel the colour coming on. You become sensitive to it and it escalates. Before you know it you're distinctly cherry red and everyone round you is going 'Ooh, look, you're blushing, you're blushing'. Which makes things ten times worse. This is usually accompanied by a sweaty feeling and your temperature going through the roof.

There are other looks. The 'Shy Di' look much used by our beloved Princess of Wales. The Wogan 'little boy lost' look when caught out by the interviewee. The wry smile used by Margaret Thatcher when she couldn't get out of a hole. The only person who never seems embarrassed is The Queen. Well, not in public anyway.

It's difficult not to spot this one as a PW; the thing is here to see the variations and how many people have perfected the trick of wriggling out of exceptionally difficult situations just by perfecting a certain look.

PALM READING AS A CHAT-UP LINE

'Do you come here often?' is the first line anyone ever thinks of when asked about common chat-up lines. Whether or not it works seems never to have been formally researched. Lines, approaches, situations – all feature heavily in how one person meets another in life. You can say it's just luck that A meets B in a given situation and they eventually end up as a couple. That may well be true but you can reduce the odds vastly by a certain amount of planning – being in the right place at the right time, knowing what to say if approached, knowing what to do if given an obvious lead and so on.

So it becomes premeditated but is there anything wrong with that? It's extremely difficult for some people even to approach other people and some people have to plan certain things just so that they don't fall apart under stress.

The whole object is to meet a person you like and progress that meeting to further meetings. Chat Up Lines sometimes work as an introduction, so does brushing past and accidentally-on-purpose touching someone. One way which works really well is to throw something of interest into the conversation.

Become an expert on palmistry. That is not difficult. Learn what a lifeline is and what all the other dents and bumps are and you're set. For some peculiar reason, palmistry impresses people. Everyone is fascinated to learn how long they're going to live, how many children they're going to have, how many husbands or wives and so on. Some people can do this for real but who cares? This is for fun and is a good way of breaking the ice to meet someone.

Almost as a by-product, you get to hold their hand as well, which is a 'territorial breakthrough'. They let you hold their hand because they don't find it threatening and you get to examine it. How you do this provides them either with a pleasant sensation or not. Either way, if it works, it moves a relationship significantly a few steps on in those initial fledgling stages.

Don't just scoff and dismiss it. Try it. It works.

PEOPLE NOT DOING ANYTHING OR SAYING WHEN SOMETHING IS WRONG

To illustrate this let's set up a scenario. You've just had a very enjoyable Big Mac and because you were starving hungry you wolfed it down like a little piggy. Because of this you have mustard mixed with tomato sauce down your front and pieces of burger and roll all over your face. Out of the store you step and you skip merrily round the shops all afternoon. Does anyone ever stop you and tell you that you look a complete jerk because you're smothered with loadsa burger stuff? No. They don't.

The result is that when you discover it much later at home you feel a complete fool at having walked around like this. The trouble is, if you saw someone like that would YOU stop and tell them? Ninety-nine times out of a hundred you wouldn't because you can't be sure how they'll react. You could end up with a smack in the teeth. So you can't really expect someone to tell you.

It's even more difficult if you have something stuck on your teeth – smiling happily at someone all day unaware that they're grimacing inwardly having to look at the remains of your breakfast or dinner – but they STILL won't tell you about it.

It's that same old problem again. It's much easier to do nothing because you don't then run any risk of being embarrassed yourself. Even to go up to a stranger and point something out to them, particularly if it will cause them temporary embarrassment, is a risk subconsciously most of us won't take.

DOORS

People get in the most horrendous muddle with doors. It's most peculiar. A door is a bit of wood or glass which fits in a hole. You open it. Walk through the hole and close it. Nothing could be more simple but what problems doors cause.

First, there is the push/pull phenomenon. If there is a door anywhere it normally opens only one way. A door which is used frequently by us, the public, will usually have a sign which says push or pull. No matter how big or small that sign, people will always do the opposite and they become very embarrassed when they eventually see the sign or it's pointed out to them.

Second, there's the 'Getting things caught in the door' phenomenon. You can guarantee that when transitting through the stiffest, most awkward doors you're usually laden down with 50 odd things in your arms. You've just about made it through this beast of a door when it closes and catches your coat, your bag, or something else in it, rendering you absolutely helpless. That, too, is particularly embarrassing as you have to be rescued.

Third, there's 'the door that won't open' phenomenon. You're standing there trying your utmost to open it and it won't. You try everything – even violence. Then someone sidles up and deftly flicks the minute catch in front of your eyes and it swings open effortlessly. A real ego killer, this.

Lift doors. How many times have you nearly been decapitated by lift doors? You think you have got them worked out and just as you go through they try to slice you in half. You can see people being positively wary of lift doors and sliding doors in general.

Finally, someone for a bit of a laugh one day invented revolving doors. This is akin to trying to jump on a moving roundabout in a children's playground without getting thrown off. The idea is satisfactory in principle and they look attractive if they're housed in the front of an impressive building but they can be a nightmare to negotiate and lethal if you get it wrong.

PEOPLE IN LIFTS

Some people don't use them because they're so frightened of them. Claustrophobia, fear of heights, fear of other people – you name it. Most of us tolerate them and everyone has a story to tell about lifts. Have you ever fantasised about being stuck in a lift overnight with someone you really fancy? Of course you have. Being equally honest, when you've been in a lift and it's suffered an unusual jerking movement, that part in the Towering Inferno film where it crashes to the floor and kills all those people has flashed through your mind, hasn't it?

The PW aspect of this is observing those around you when in a lift. All kinds of things happen. It jerks midway down on its journey and you all look nervously at each other. A man and a woman in a lift on their own will always stand as far away from each other as they can. You always have a little snigger to yourself when someone else almost gets cut in half by the doors.

You will enjoy the look on the faces of the people left behind when you've entered a full lift and they haven't. You get butterflies in your stomach when more people cram into a lift than the recommended number – and you're in it as well.

When there are four of you in a lift and somebody farts, everyone looks accusingly at everyone else – quickly if it's audible, slowly if it's silent but deadly.

People always strike up the most inane conversations in lifts because they feel they have to say something.

'Hot, isn't it?'

'Nice day, isn't it?'

And so on.

Then there's the annoyance of waiting for a lift for ages when you've pushed the button. Or of it stopping on a number of floors before it reaches yours. Or of it going up when you want it to go down. Or of it not coming at all and you end up walking down trillions of stairs.

A good invention, lifts.

GETTING OUT OF CARS

It's a favourite photo opportunity for photographers from magazines and tabloid newspapers. It's almost a form of perversion as they wait outside the doors to cars for a famous celebrity, usually female, to emerge and embarrass themselves in the process.

The shot for which they're hoping and praying is known as the 'triangle' shot in the trade. That split second where a woman gets out of a car in a tight dress or skirt, one foot on the ground, the other in the car, and a glimpse of knickers becomes visible between either leg and the stretched top of the dress/skirt. The shot they all desperately want is a picture of the Princess of Wales caught in this position. It has yet to be photographed but when it is the photographer will be able to retire, as such a shot would sell for a six-figure sum at least. Sick maybe but not if you're the photographer who walks away with the money perhaps. After all, he just takes the picture. What the purchaser does with it is up to them.

Number two is the Duchess of York and you will recall that she has already been snapped getting out of a car showing thighs up to a dangerously high level. If they can't get the 'triangle' the paparazzi will normally go for the thigh shot. This ensures good 'pun' headlines like 'The thighs the limit' or 'Thigh high' or 'A sight for sore thighs'.

It's not all confined to women, as people make such asses of themselves getting out of cars. Many notable men have been photographed falling or stumbling un-ceremoniously out of vehicles in shots which have circulated round the world.

Every day, in every street, people show themselves up because they cannot work out a way to get out of a car with a modicum of dignity. The older you get the worse it becomes. Perhaps car designers deliberately make cars like this for a laugh but no-one, from royalty downwards, appears to have mastered this seemingly simple task.

ADDICTIONS

Say this title to most people and they will immediately think of drugs. Obvious really – you take drugs; you become addicted. Everyone knows that but addiction in its most basic form is when you can't do without something. Sometimes it's easy to see, sometimes you'd be surprised by an addiction.

People can become addicted to their partner, sometimes obsessively. They simply can't be without them. If, for any reason, they are without them they become moody, sulky or downright depressed. They develop scenarios in their mind – their partner is having an affair, for example – and an untreated partner addiction can have a horrible ending.

Coffee and tea are other common addictions. Check one day on either yourself or someone whom you can monitor closely. See how many mugs of coffee or tea you or they drink in a day. Work it out over a week. Then try and make them or yourself go without any coffee or tea for a whole week. You'll soon see how addictive even a simple drink can be. You may find you can't go a week without one, which is frightening.

Other addictions are common. The slightest twinge of a headache and people reach for the paracetamol. When they get a real headache they need to take more to overcome the resistance the body has built up. They HAVE to have the tablets around just in case. Cream cakes are a common addiction. You see one and you just HAVE to have it. Sweets in a sweet shop. You pop in for a magazine or a paper and because you have a subconscious addiction to, say, a Mars bar, you find yourself automatically picking up one whether you want it or not.

Very easy to observe as a PW exercise, the ultimate has to be sex. Many researchers and scientists reckon that it is possible to become addicted to sex if it becomes habitual; and when it stops for whatever reason, those same side effects of depression and moodiness are prevalent.

SOCIAL EVENINGS – PEOPLE NOT LEAVING

It's a situation which happens to everyone at some stage or another, no matter what kind of life you lead. You decide to invite a few friends for the evening and you've gone to great lengths to get everything correct. You've planned the meal carefully, checking peoples' likes and dislikes, worked out seating arrangements so that 'enemies' aren't on each others' laps all evening, and you've even bought a special bottle of wine.

Everyone turns up, some later than others, and the evening progresses well. A good time is invariably had by all if you overlook one or two little faux pas during the night.

How does it end? If you have a reasonably large dinner party with nobody staying overnight, it can be amusing.

Scenario 1 is where one couple makes their excuse to be off, and amid much kissing and hand shaking, they depart. Within five minutes you then find everyone else has gone too, as each couple finds their own respective excuses. A sudden end to a good evening but at least you can now go to bed.

Scenario 2 is when people won't leave. You've all had a good evening and all your guests have drunk you virtually dry and it's now becoming a trifle extended; 2am comes and goes; 3am comes and goes. How do you get rid of them?

This is the PW bit. Look out for the little tricks people employ. The nudging. The kick under the table. The winking between the host couple. The broad hint... 'Oh, my goodness, look at the time' with a greatly exaggerated look at the watch. Usually people take the hint by this time but some people still hang on. 'Oh, yes it's late, isn't it?' One more drink and then we'll make a move, eh?' So you find yourself making yet another pot of coffee.

At 4am it's getting a little desperate. What do you do? Turn off the lights and go to bed leaving them there? Pick them up and put them outside? Or stay there hoping they'll go any minute, while making a mental note not to invite them again for a long, long time. I suspect most of us do the latter.

FOOTSY

Far better than any chat-up line or planned approach, this must be the easiest way of finding whether or not someone fancies you. It is also one of the most dangerous. If you've never played it you've missed out. Is it 'illegal'? Possibly. It's certainly flirting; and it can also be very embarrassing if the other person doesn't want to know.

To play this game you need two feet, although one will do. Make sure you're sitting reasonably near the person you intend to 'check out' when you sit down for a meal or whatever.

Start by making a gentle brush with your foot against theirs. That will produce one of two responses. They will either move their foot away instantly so that it doesn't happen again or they will leave it there assuming your brush was a mistake. If they've moved their foot away you have to go 'looking' for it, which makes the second brush more obvious. If they move away again you're starting to get on to dodgy ground. If they leave their foot there again you could be making headway.

At the third attempt the stakes begin to escalate. If they're not interested you are now likely to get a response. This will either be a forceful removal of the foot followed by a glare, or a kick followed by a glare. You would best be advised to give up at this point. A third response is the loud statement by them 'Are you trying to play footsy with me?' which is mega-embarrassing because you've then been caught out, your partner look daggers at you and you know you will have some grief later. This also effectively ends the game.

If, however, they're interested, you will also get a response at this point. Their foot will twitch slightly in reply. They may brush back at you. Or you may get a knowing look. You are now in the danger stakes as the look may be spotted. People may sense the movement of feet under the table. Or the wrong person may get brushed.

From then it's down to the kind of person you are and how brave you are. Make a wrong move and you could end up without a partner, getting your teeth smashed in, or losing every friend you have. It's all best treated as a little lighthearted fun. If it becomes more serious you'll have problems.

HOSTILE ROAD WORKERS AT TEMPORARY TRAFFIC LIGHTS

Temporary Traffic Lights (TTL) are really a product of the 80s. As roads begin to sink, break up and generally die under the increasing weight of traffic, TTL have sprung up everywhere. We all know about cones. They are the scourge of modern life. It isn't possible to go ANYWHERE without spotting them but cones are negotiable. Even if you have to drive over them. TTL are not negotiable. They are a symbol of power. A symbol of authority. They say 'I can tell you what to do. If I say stop, you STOP'.

There is nowhere TTL cannot be put. If you are the owner of a set of TTL you can put them anywhere you wish. The normal practice is to place them just out of vision round a tight bend so that you have to put your foot through the floor as you go round the bend to avoid hitting everyone; and you cannot beat them.

At 4am with no-one around, a set of TTL will be green as you approach them. Just as you are approaching the point of no return they change to red. So, because you're an honest citizen you stop. They stay red indefinitely and you fume. Until you finally get out and rant and rave at the little box which is supposed to detect the presence of your car.

Equally annoying is when you're sitting patiently in a long queue at a set of TTL. Roadworkers in the coned-off bit stand and glare at you with pure hatred. How DARE you clog up their bit of road while they're working? How DARE you even use that route without asking them first? How DARE you transit their little zone without stopping your car and giving them £50 for the privilege of doing so?

Keep your eyes open next time you approach a set of TTL and you'll see for yourself.

WINKING AT PEOPLE

Another practical one, this. It's something you can try wherever you are and whatever you're doing. It was big in the 30s and 40s – the war years. People, it is reckoned, were far more friendly then and far less self-conscious. They did not worry what other people thought of them so much. Cameraderie was the name of the game.

Winking. Even the 'sound' of the word makes some people snigger now but it's such an easy thing to do. Yet there are people who can't do it.

There used to be such a thing as the knowing wink. You would wink at someone as if to signify that you knew what they're trying to say. Lovers would wink at each other as a kind of secret signal. A man would wink at a woman he found attractive and receive a pleasant smile by return as a thank-you for the compliment.

Nowadays, a wink seems to have become something seedy. Or smutty. 'Nudge, nudge, wink, wink' seems to convey an air of seediness which is a little sad. It's synonymous with the Sid James Carry On films era, which today are considered to have been a 'bad thing' by the theorists.

So try it for yourself. Wink at someone. Boldly. Secretly. Shyly. Shrewdly. Or for no reason at all and just see what reaction you get.

People will probably think you have a nervous affliction and ask if you're alright. Or they'll think you're being saucy and reprimand you. Very few will wink back at you.

WHISTLING

Very similar to winking. It hails from the same war years era and it was the kind of action which symbolised chirpiness, happiness and a good nature. The image of the milkman whistling a little tune as he went about his business is an endearing one which most people can identify fairly easily but why don't people whistle nowadays?

Like winking, whistling is very simple but there are many people who can't do it. Perhaps, as we've all become more self-conscious, we're frightened of looking silly. After all, to whistle you have to contort your mouth and some people look positively daft when they try to whistle. That didn't worry people 50 years ago but it does now.

What do people do now if they find someone whistling away? Generally, they get irritated by it. They'll put up with it for a time and eventually they'll say something. Usually it's something very sarcastic and the other person soon stops. If a person is whistling because they're content and they're told to stop, it shatters that happy disposition. It seems to be alright to go round singing to yourself, or even talking to yourself, but whistling is a no-no.

Again, try it for yourself – if you can. When you're feeling happy, start whistling and see what reaction you get. It'll show you just how much people have changed in the last 50 years.

MUTTON DRESSED AS LAMB

A PW which again is very easy to spot. When you do you'll be surprised at how many people are unaware how they look. It's not so much to do with dress sense but more with people trying to look younger than they are. Men and women are equally at fault but it's probably more obvious in women.

Out socially is the most obvious place. The 39-year-old woman who should really be dressed in couture clothes turns up in the latest skintight shorty dress with suspender nobbles showing through. White high-heeled stilettos round off the bottom end while the bottom is contained precariously in the skimpiest knickers which show through the dress. Bangles jingle on either arm and the earrings would make a perfect pair of chandeliers over a dining table in a stately home. You can sniff her a mile away as she wears teenage perfume and her make-up is plastered on thickly to fill in the various lines, furrows and crows legs — let alone feet. The hair is 'natural' peroxide blonde.

Our mutton male looks equally ridiculous. Trousers three sizes too small mean that a voluminous belly wobbles around unsupported over the top of the belt and it swings left to right as he walks. It's about all that does swing as **that** is contained so tightly in a posing pouch it's a wonder it doesn't get gangrene.

Italian loafer shoes look reasonably satisfactory but a little out of place on this overweight specimen and the shirt is neatly arranged with the blouson effect to hide the midriff bulges. A pert rear end there isn't; rather the seam down the middle of the trousers struggling to hold itself together.

A huge imitation Rolex watch adorns the left wrist and much hair adorns the forearms and chest. Nowadays not even male muttons wear medallions but the chain is still there. Aftershave reeks for metres round our male and there's usually a cute little moustache to top off the whole lot. Invariably, our male mutton is half bald.

Remind you of anyone you've seen lately?

STONE-CLADDING

Most of us take pride in our homes. If you own it, it is, after all, your single most expensive material possession. Maintenance is done eventually, if not willingly. Decoration occurs whenever. Lawns get mowed. Gardens get weeded – sometimes. But generally, we're proud of our homes.

Why is it then that some people go berserk? Is it a mental condition? Some people take a delight in painting their house pink, or yellow, or green, or some other weird colour. Other people fit replacement double glazed windows totally out of character with the property. And yet others build on extensions over garages that look like some kind of giant wart growing on the side of the house.

But it all pales into insignificance when you look at a row of terraced houses. There they are, sitting neatly side by side quite happily, when AAAARGH! Right in the middle of a block of 14 you see one that stands out a mile. It is the home of the stone cladder.

What on earth possesses someone to go out and buy 30 tons of paving slab-type bricks, 2,000 tubes of glue, a big ladder, and a slab cutting machine? And having done that, what bizarre combination of brain cells then makes them go and stick them over the outside walls of their house? Who are these people? Where do they come from? What do they look like?

'Well, it improves the insulation, doesn't it?'

'Makes it individual, doesn't it?'

'Adds to the value of the property, doesn't it?'

'Gives the place a bit of class, doesn't it?'

No. It doesn't. It looks utterly stupid.

THE BLOOD DONOR

Let's say at the beginning of this one that this is not meant to decry blood donors. They are humane, caring people who want to help others and without them people involved in accidents or illnesses would die. So, let's not hear a word against them. It is to be encouraged. Why then do some of us, including the author, find it the most frightening prospect?

The thought of going voluntarily into a blood donor unit fills some of us with dread. Walking voluntarily up to a bed and lying on it thinking that your last moment has come. A nurse comes up to you and gives you a little prick. This may or may not appeal to you but they have to do it to check your blood isn't full of nasty little poxes, viruses and the like.

Subject to your body passing this test they then ask you to bare your arm. It is disinfected with a swab and then a spear is plunged into it, usually accompanied by the words 'This won't hurt'. Whether or not it does is largely irrelevant by now as you see your blood pulsing out down a tube to be collected in a bag. You have only eight pints of it in your body, so your life is in the hands of someone who has to guess when they've milked enough from you.

What if the phone rings while you're leaking? There they are chatting to their friend on the phone while your bag is overflowing on the floor and you turn a brighter shade of white. Finally, you're left lying flat like a piece of paper as all the blood has drained out of you. A bit special, eh? What if you don't stop leaking when they take out the spear? What if it starts spurting again on the bus home? The person next to you is scarcely likely to be impressed.

Blood donors are very special people. Thoughts like this don't worry them. They care enough for others to ignore all this. Some of them go so regularly they must be running on blood vapour in their veins now. Their arm is also full of holes. Professionals have had a one-way valve fitted.

It makes them very easy to spot. They're also a little tubby because they get a free biscuit after each draining.

HAMSTER OWNERS

There can be nothing so useless in this world as a hamster. It is brain dead. It is pathetic. It sits there. Eats. Sleeps. Drinks. And dies. More advanced versions of hamsters can, after considerable training, be made to run inside a wheel to make it go round. Owners are known to have thrown lavish parties after such an event to celebrate.

Why someone should want to own a hamster as a pet has defied eminent psychiatrists for decades. There are so many pets from which to choose – cats, dogs, fish, children, tarantulas which at least frighten people, rabbits, birds, ants. So why do people choose a hamster?

Let's look at its aesthetic qualities. It's furry, so it's cute. It's small, so it's cheap. It doesn't live long, so it's expendable. It has little legs, so it can't run far. There it ends.

A hamster is a mutant rat. Must be. It look similar, acts similar – it's just never had a book written about it. All it needs to survive is a tiny cage, some straw, a water bottle and a doting owner.

The method is simple. Buy a hamster and a cage. Take home. Put hamster in cage. Feed. Bury it one month later. It's in that month that hamster owners excel. They can be found talking to their pride and joy, urging it to do exciting things like stand up and sit down. They read poems to it. Tell it bedtime stories. Shriek with delight when it opens and shuts its eyes. Hold a birthday party when it survives the first week and go positively ga ga when it wakes up successfully next morning.

Watch for a hamster owner in your environment. They are outwardly normal people but what do they do at home? What are they really like?

SEE-THROUGH CLOTHING

One of life's little oddities and it mainly concerns women. In the spring, as the sun starts to shine a little, we all cast off our winter woollies and reveal pasty-looking white limbs which darken gradually in the sun. As summer arrives, more and more is revealed and again darkens gradually until we all turn into adorable-looking bronzed objects. That's the theory anyhow.

Yet, even when we're fully bronzed and looking good, some occasions demand slightly more formal wear than others; you can't really arrive for a dinner party or social event in a swimsuit, can you?

We all tend to wear light-colour clothes in the summer – invariably white. It is a fact of life that white clothes for women seem to be made of thinner material than men's. No, you have to accept it. It's a fact.

When you dress to go out it's your choice what to wear. Presumably you check just before you depart that you look OK. Why, then, do women get so upset when someone points out to them that what they're wearing is totally see-through?

'You shouldn't be looking' is the usual reply. How can you NOT look? Men look at women; women look at men. If a woman is going to walk around with see-through clothes, who isn't going to look? Presumably if the wearer didn't want people to look they wouldn't wear stuff that's see-through in the first place, would they?

Is it, in fact, a modern-day form of exhibitionism and then getting very uppity on discovery so that people don't think it's a bit tarty?

YAWNING

Normally associated with tiredness, yawning is a reaction over which most of us appear to have no control. It's supposed to be a way of getting extra oxygen into your body to combat fatigue. How and why we yawn only doctors can explain but one unexplained action associated with yawning fits neatly into this PW book.

You may or may not have noticed but yawning in public has some remarkable side-effects. First, it's rude to yawn without putting your hand over your mouth. Ask your mum but how many of us do it?

Second, there normally isn't a singular yawn. Yawns come in multiples, not singular instances. Yawn once and you'll do it again very quickly, perhaps without even realising it. Third, and most interesting, yawning is auto-suggestive. Try yawning when there are people around you and very quickly someone else near you will also yawn. Followed very quickly by someone else. Now why should this be?

Conversely, if you're in a group and someone yawns, you'll probably end up yawning as well. Why? You're not tired, you feel fine. Yet you end up yawning.

There's probably a very good reason but I can't think what it is. Can you? There's no doubt, however, that it works, even if you have to fake a yawn to start it off. It doesn't have to be a real 'over-the-top'-type stretchy yawn either.

SCRATCHING

Very similar to yawning; this, too, leads to auto-suggestion in groups of people. Scratching is, however, very different in concept from yawning. You yawn when you're tired. You scratch when you have an itch. And you itch only because a.) you have a spot or b.) some molecular bug is eating into you causing the itch.

Both a.) and b.) carry connotations of 'uncleanliness', so scratching in its way becomes 'not nice'. Sit in a group of people constantly scratching yourself and someone will eventually ask if you're OK.

Scratching therefore is socially uncomfortable. We've covered scratching in embarrassing places elsewhere in this book but scratching *per se* is equally interesting.

Again, try it for yourself. When you're out with people, start scratching yourself. Very soon someone WILL ask you if you're OK. Also other people will start scratching themselves for no reason. Subconsciously, they've seen you scratching and assumed that you have whole battalions of fleas and other horrors under your clothes marching up and down – and that makes them scratch, too.

Equally, if someone else is scratching you, too, will find yourself doing the same – even if you're the cleanest person around and you've never scratched in your life.

There's a third aspect. While you've been reading this page it's a fair bet that you've scratched yourself somewhere on your body, simply because of the suggestion of itching, fleas and so on. You're probably not even aware that you've done it.

COUPLES PLAYFULLY TOUCHING
EACH OTHER

If you've read through this book continuously until now without skipping pages you're halfway through. You'll already have some idea now of what the basic art-form of PW is all about – observing anything and everything about you. As you can see, it's not difficult and it's not voyeuristic – just interesting. You've probably been able to think up some of your own as things that you've read here have suggested others to you. Good. You're well on the way.

Let's turn our attentions now to couples. Two people meet. They like each other. They have sex. They fall in love. Some fall in love first and have sex after but that's not under discussion here. The longer couples last, the more they grow like each other. You can see it all the time. He starts mimicking her. She starts acting like him, and so on.

Another thing which couples are very good at developing are unspoken codes. They get to know instinctively when the other wants to do something by certain looks, body actions, caresses. It's those which can be interesting, particularly if they're your friends.

One of the more embarrassing things you can be caught doing is tweaking or touching playfully your partners more private parts. Perhaps you're lusting, perhaps you're drunk, or perhaps you're just being secretive but you do it anyway. Perhaps it's an unspoken code between you.

Whatever, it isn't half embarrassing when someone sees you doing it. It takes a good deal of explaining away. The worst possible scenario of all is when it's your or their parents who catch you.

HOW TO SPOT SOMEONE IN LOVE

You may think this is easy but it's not. Does anyone seriously walk around being sick in the mornings any more? Not eating any food? Drawing pink hearts all over the place? Of course not. Things are far more subtle nowadays.

The most interesting 'cases' to observe are people you suspect of forming a relationship, clandestine or otherwise. People can fall in love over a reasonably long period of time through being together a great deal. One minute they're friends, the next minute they're in love. So how do you tell when they have in fact 'fallen'?

Friends take the mickey out of each other constantly. Early lovers don't for fear of upsetting each other. Fun between two people gives way to lingering looks and unfailing support. One easy test is to say something slightly disconcerting about a person when their suspected lover is around. A friend will join in the fun; a lover will jump to their support – a dead giveaway.

Both people you suspect will also appear more revitalised than of late. One or the other may well have discovered new interests. One or the other may have embarked recently on a 'keep-fit' campaign to the surprise of everyone and you find that one or the other suddenly becomes far more tolerant towards people about whom they previously got very uptight. It's because they have another interest now previous things which seemed important to them aren't nearly so vital.

At work is the easiest place to see this. More and more people are now meeting at work, because everyone is working harder and longer. Thus, outside meeting opportunities are much reduced. Lingering conversation over the photocopier, around the drinks machine and by the loos are sure signs that they're not just discussing the weather or Diana in accounts any more.

BLESS YOU

Have you ever noticed what everyone says whenever you sneeze? You may not have done but it's simple. They say Bless You. What an odd thing to say. When you cough does anyone say anything? No. When you break wind does anyone say anything? No. So why do they feel compelled to turn to religion when you sneeze?

It's an old custom going back to The Great Plague and it shows how even in the 1990s we still stick by traditions dating back hundreds of years without even realising why we do it.

Think of the old song Ring 'o Roses. That came from the time of The Great Plague.

Ring 'o Ring 'o Roses

A Pocket full of Posies

Atishoo, Atishoo

We all fall down.

We're all taught it as children almost 400 years after it was developed. Why? Because successive generations have been indoctrinated with it, stemming originally from a terrible fear.

Sneezing was one of the main symptoms of The Plague. When you'd sneezed three times invariably you'd die. There was no cure for The Plague. So when someone sneezed at the time whoever was closest would administer a kind of 'last rites' and 'bless' the person who was not long for this world.

That's why, without knowing WHY we do it, we still all say 'Bless you' nowadays, 400 years on.

As a footnote, many of the people who died in The Great Plague were buried in mass graves at Blackheath in London, under the heath area which is now grassed over. That's how Black Heath got its name.

er...
right...
OK...
actually...

MANNERISMS

The very easiest of People Watchings to do. Everyone has mannerisms. The kind of individual touches which make you the person you are. Very often you are unaware of them but everyone else is only too aware of them. After all, they see you daily and that's part of how they see you.

What are mannerisms? Picking your nose is one which horrifies most people who do it because they don't realise that they do. Others may have you marked down as a nose picker – all your friends may even call you it when you're not around – but you don't realise it.

Scratching or tugging your ear is another common one, as is a deft 'wipe' or brush of your nose every few minutes with your hand. Others are little twitches, nervous or otherwise. You may stand up or sit down a certain way which people might find strange and mark down as a mannerism.

Your speech may be peppered with 'dogwords' – another common mannerism. Dogwords are meaningless little words with which you punctuate your speech, usually the same word each time. That's your mannerism. You use dogwords automatically when speaking to give your mouth time to catch up with what your brain is telling you. Examples of common dogwords are 'er', 'right', 'OK', 'actually' and so on.

Tugging or twisting your hair is a mannerism. Fidgeting with a pen or pencil is another. Picking your nails. Biting your nails. Crossing or uncrossing your legs. Kicking off your shoes and playing with them. Constantly interrupting others while they're talking or saying 'yes', 'yes' every few seconds is a very common mannerism. Also, people who finish sentences of other people who are talking.

You can probably think of many more. There's nothing wrong with any of them. It just makes you, or anyone else, who they are.

TRAINS

Another great place to spot all kinds of behaviour. People become very territorial when travelling on trains, especially if they take the same train at the same time every day. Woe betide anyone who sits in THEIR seat one day. It ruins their whole week.

It's a good place to spot Creatures of Habit (see earlier). On trains people tend to do exactly the same things at the same times every journey. Out comes the paper at a certain station. A review of papers for work at another and so on.

Have you ever noticed how nobody talks on trains? A compartment can be full of people who don't know each other but nobody talks to anyone else. If someone tries to strike up a conversation they are very much frowned on.

People become very moral on trains. If someone dares to light a cigarette in a no smoking compartment, it's war. Couples kissing on trains are frowned on. Couples going further are positively outlawed.

Who among us has never thought of pulling the communication cord just once to see what would happen and to hell with the fine? It's that feeling of power again. 'Heh, heh. I can stop a train'.

People find the most extraordinary things about which to argue. Should we have the heater on or off? Should we have the window open or not? Shouldn't we have the lights on? Who sits where? Who wants to be by the window? Who wants to travel backwards? Are we or aren't we on the proper train? Are we or aren't we in the correct part of the train?

Train behaviour is a subject in its own right as people who use trains regularly seem to develop their own micro-personalities. A PW field trip for a day could be no worse spent than by buying a train ticket.

AIRPLANES

If people's behaviour on trains is strange, it's positively mind-boggling on airplanes. Aircraft have been with us for some 60-odd years but the way some people go on you'd think they were invented yesterday. On every flight there's always the drunk. The one who thinks it's macho to drink the aircraft dry, not realising the effect alcohol has on you at 30,000 feet.

Then there's the person who professes very loudly to be the founder of the 'mile high' club. This, if you don't know, is the 'club' for those who have somehow managed to bonk someone else with one hand wrapped around the sink, one foot on the ceiling, one arm down the loo, and the other leg holding the door shut of a 2 foot by 2 foot aircraft loo. The person normally who's most vociferous about this would run a mile if anyone even showed the slightest interest in going to the loo with them. Most people, however, are far too busy whingeing about everything even to think about sex.

'The seats are too small'

'There's not enough legroom'

'I can't see the screen'

'The food's awful'

'The hostess is an ugly old bitch'

'Delays. Turbulence. Air blowers. Headphones. Luggage Space.'

You name it. They whinge about it.

Then there's the fountains of eternal knowledge. They know what makes an aircraft go up, down, sideways, land, take-off, and the limits and conditions in which it all happens. Megabores.

The navigator. They always know where you are to half an inch anywhere in the world. They will delight in showing you Greece out of the window when all anyone else can see is sky and clouds.

Finally there's the seasoned traveller. The frequent flyer. The one who's been around the world 50 times in a year. Mr or Mrs Corporate. In fact, they fly about twice a year – Benidorm and Geneva – but they know everything there is to know about flying. How to fly it, type of aircraft, configurations, how to bed a hostess in Mombasa – you name it, they've done it. Frightening people.

TWENTY-SIX MINUTES

Only in the last few years have people mustered the courage to start talking openly about sex. In the 60s, if you believe the hype, everybody did it but few people talked about it. In the 70s people did it but were a little shy about admitting it. In the 80s people stopped doing it because they were warned of dire consequences if they did.

Now, everybody talks about it. In perspective. People are far more scientific about it now. It's more how, and why, and how frequent. It's virtually impossible to pick up a magazine and not find a survey about something to do with sex in it.

Yet, until very recently no-one had ever broached the question about how long 'the sex act' was supposed to last. Five minutes? An hour? All day? Nobody dared ask for fear of feeling 'inferior'.

Last year, however, a team of experts funded by a government grant from some university or other did ask. They asked a representative sample of people from across the U.K. So the result can be deemed to be reasonably accurate.

The question was: 'When you engage in sex, how long on average does it last?' The overall answer was 26 minutes.

That seems like a fairly long time to me. To make it an average, there must be plenty of couples who pound away for some two hours or more to compensate for the five-minute wonders.

So who are those average 26-minuters? How do they manage to last so long with the children about, the washing machine going, the phone ringing, the thing splitting and so on? Look around you. See if you can tell. Look for the signs.

More worrying is that the same team of experts did the same survey again this year. Asking the same question. This time the overall answer was 23 minutes. So where has the missing three minutes gone?

PEOPLE IN CARS

People in cars live in a world of their own. They get into a car and they're off. People change character when they get behind the wheel. Even the meekest and mildest person can be an absolute terror on a dual carriageway. People hate it when overtaken. They actually put their foot down to try to stop it, even if they've been travelling slowly previously. They sit hunched up over the steering wheel, their face set in a mask of concentration looking straight ahead.

Then there's a boy racer. Nobody beats him at the lights. He sits there and revs and revs – until vroom! He's gone. Normally if you just poodle off slowly he gets embarrassed and gives up to try someone else. Girls are not much better. They race around country lanes at 80mph, totally oblivious to anything coming the other way. Normally they're doing their make-up as well.

The flash car owner. They sit posing at every opportunity, raising and lowering the windows to impress you, leaning with one elbow on the window ledge, making sure you turn a darker shade of green.

The personalised registration number owner. They forget that most people have cottoned on now to the fact that they have one only because they can't afford a new car. The three-wheeler owner. Not long for this world. The Skoda or Lada owner. Not of this world.

The habits of people in cars are disgusting. They pick their noses. They shout abuse at you. They make rude signs. They throw things out of the window. They hit you in car parks. They cut you up. They never indicate what they're going to do.

Finally, people in cars are always trying to do two things at once. Steering and changing gear. Steering and changing the radio. Steering and opening the sun-roof, adjusting the mirror, wing mirrors, seat, stereo. Real flash individuals steer, change gear, play with the radio, play with the on-board computer, talk on the phone, answer the fax, and talk to the person next to them all at once – while driving at 95mph on a motorway.

UMBRELLAS

A simple enough device. Something portable and easy to operate which keeps you dry outside when it rains. Easy – but fraught with problems. They never work when you need them quickly. No matter what design you have they ALWAYS stick when it's pouring with rain. No matter what direction you hold it you'll always get wet. No matter how big it is you'll never have enough room underneath it.

Nowadays there are millions of designs. Companies give them away if you buy a product. Usually insurance companies. Has anyone ever collected a set? Golfing umbrellas are popular at the moment because of their size. They also look pretty because they're always in bright colours. They're good for stabbing people as well but they stick like any other; it's more embarrassing, too, because they're bigger and everyone notices. Portable jobs are easier to store but they tend to turn inside out in the wind and they're usually black, which is pretty boring.

The real fun comes when there's two of you. Real good rainy day PW, this. A tall man and a short women under an umbrella. She gets wet; he stays dry. Two people under a too small umbrella? They both get wet. Two people walking towards each other, brollies down... CRASH. A horrendous tangle and they both get wet. New out this year is the stereo umbrella. Two shafts at 45 degrees to each other and two canopies. A good idea – it just looks daft but at least you stay dry.

Coming soon – the transparent umbrella. It hangs all around you and you look through it. It keeps you dry to your waist but it still means cars can splash you.

How many times have you spotted an umbrella minus its owner? Left to die on its own. Forgotten. Unloved. Until someone nicks it.

WHAT PEOPLE DO WHEN CONCENTRATING

Some people daydream. Some people can't concentrate if they try. Others enter a different world and are impossible to disturb but all display exceptional signs.

There's the pen chewer. Usually someone else's. When you get it back it's covered in teeth marks all over the end, with half the plastic missing. Presumably it's inside the other person.

The vacant look. They can be looking straight at you and you could be standing there starkers but they wouldn't notice. They have the exceptional ability to switch off their eyes whilst open.

The tongue out of the corner of the mouth. Very common this; we've probably all done it at some time. In nasty situations though, when surprised, you can end up biting it and it's very painful.

The thoughtful rubbing of the chin. More in movies really; you don't see it much in real life.

Doodling. Not part of daydreaming as some people would think; more an abstract aid to concentration. Psychologists are supposed to be able to tell what kind of person you are by your doodles but don't we all draw arrows, boxes, flowers, names and patterns?

The busy look. Totally absorbed in whatever they're doing. Oblivious to the world. Just getting on with it. These types don't even notice a phone ringing.

That's six. You could easily double it yourself by watching those around you. If you're reading this on the beach, I think you're probably excused.

PEOPLE IN SUITS IN HOT WEATHER

It's a peculiar British disease. In hot countries round the world, men and women have their own outfits that they wear day in, day out. They remain comfortable 24 hours a day. In the United States, most people work in air-conditioned offices but they, too, wear lightweight clothes throughout the day, usually shorts.

In Britain, it's acceptable for women to wear what they like in hot weather. Usually as little and as thin as possible and they stay cool. It's business and socially acceptable for a woman to arrive in virtually anything so long as it's decent.

So why is it different for men? Why does a man have to overheat in hot weather to comply with convention? He has to wear underwear – and a vest if he lives with his mum – socks, closed shoes, trousers, shirt, tie and a jacket. In all kinds of hot weather. Why isn't it socially acceptable for a man to go to a business meeting wearing thin shorts and a polo-type, short-sleeved thin shirt?

They do it in the Navy. Officers and commanders look exceptionally smart parading round the decks of their ships in crisp white shorts and pressed shirts. They do it in the Army, too.

So, if it's good enough for the service boys, why are the vast majority of British men made to sweat it out for the sake of convention? Can you imagine the howls of abuse and derision which would greet the brave man daring to turn up for a board meeting in a pair of shorts one day?

Spot a poor overheating British male in the next heatwave and take sympathy on him.

It's tough being a man. Mind you, why do some men wear nothing but vests or T-shirts when out shopping in the snow? You see that, too. Daft.

WOMEN IN SHORT SKIRTS

There is a school of thought which says hemlines on skirts go up or down according to the nation's economic climate at the time. Witness the long hemlines of the 30s and 40s. The short skirts of the 60s. Longer in the 70s. Short again in the late 80s. It's probably true.

A woman in a short skirt is a number one eyecatcher for men. Most women who wear short skirts have the legs for it and look stunning. Some don't but at least they have the bottle to try. That's not what's under discussion here. What is being looked at is the reaction a woman in a short skirt causes.

Consider a scene in a pub. Two men sit drinking with their two women partners. In strolls a young woman wearing a pelmet – a very short dress or skirt. What happens?

a.)   Both men look instantly, as if magnetised. Equally quickly both men realise that they shouldn't be looking and avert their gaze to anything else in the room, as far away from the woman as possible while still trying to sneak a look and talking about something else. They're also hoping their women didn't spot the initial look. They daren't comment on how nice she is.

b.)   Both women will look at each other and say the same thing, 'What a tart'. She could be the most stunning woman in the world but both women will describe her as a tart, qualifying the statement by saying that only a tart would wear such clothing in a pub.

The men are fighting their natural instincts. The women immediately go on the defensive. Why? You might think this is stereotyped and sexist but it's true. Watch it for yourself.

SURGEONS

You might think that a train driver is a weird occupation. Or a nuclear power worker. Or perhaps a jeweller. Or an estate agent. But a surgeon? What happens to a person in their formative years which makes them want to cut up bodies for a living when they're in their thirties? Is it the desire to cure people? Is it that childlike desire to take things apart just to see how they're made – then put them back together again? Or is it something far more sinister?

A surgeon is very much like a butcher. A butcher cuts up things when they're dead. A surgeon cuts them up when they're alive. It's a good job we have them or a few of us might not be reading this now but could you do that job?

How do you train? You could study all the theory in the world but sooner or later you have to stick your very first knife into someone and if you get it wrong – like most of us do in our first job – the poor patient bears your slash marks for ever. What if your first bit of stitching goes a bit skew-wiffy? Nice row of dots over the old bikini line.

Supposing you've had a bad night and you go into the operating theatre in a huff. 'What have we today, nurse? Four lungs, two legs, one testicle and an appendix?'

Supposing, just supposing, you have a momentary lapse of concentration? You whip off the wrong bit. You can scarcely stick it back on, or in again, can you?

Can you imagine standing there holding someone's heart in your hand going b,boom, b,boom... and examining it for pock marks... and checking the valves are all OK? 'Alright nurse, I think it's OK. Stuff it back in and let's sew 'em up'.

Something must make these people choose their profession. How do you tell if someone is a surgeon out socially? Are they looking at you for your beauty or are they lusting after your intestines? Do they carry a scalpel in their pocket for an emergency?

Pretty scary stuff, eh? Perhaps we'd rather not know.

AMATEUR SOLICITORS

It must be said that real solicitors train very hard. They are swots at school. They take O and A levels. Not for them the GCSE. They go to university. They drink a great deal. They get a degree. They go to law school. They come out with their qualification. Then they become solicitors and life stops at 30 because they're always so tired but at least they can do their job. Or they make out they can. It might take them weeks to do one single thing and £100 for a letter is eminently reasonable nowadays but they get results.

Not so the amateur solicitors. There's usually one in every social circle. The one who knows it all.

Matrimonial dispute? 'Let me handle the divorce for you. I'll save your a fortune.'

Moving house? 'Conveyancy. No problem. 50 quid. I'll do it for you tonight'.

Wee bit of litigation against the garage which has destroyed your car? 'Leave them to me. I've got a great track record with garages. They won't stand a chance. We'll sue them in the Old Bailey.'

An amateur solicitor will always be very vocal about this or that they've done in the past. When you press them on specifics and ask for the teeniest bit of proof they start making excuses and their advice is nearly always wrong.

Amateur solicitors wear loud clothes. Real ones wear boring clothes. Amateur solicitors use big words which sound legal. Real solicitors don't understand big words because they communicate only by letter and they look up words in their big books first. Amateur solicitors are always available with advice. You can never reach a real solicitor. Amateur solicitors will always return your calls. Real ones don't.

See if you can spot the difference.

CUSTOMS HALLS AT AIRPORTS

You come off the aircraft. Weary after a long flight. Everyone is equal. You follow the signs to passport control. It takes ages to get through because you can't find the 'U.K. residents' sign. Eventually you give up looking and go through the European Community Nationals channel. So far, so good.

You proceed to baggage claim after your carousel number comes up on the screen. 'KT384 Malaga. Baggage Claim 2.' You find a trolley. The wheel squeaks. It drives crookedly. No matter. You're nearly home.

You gaze expectantly at every piece of luggage which emerges from the tunnel, praying that it's yours. More and more comes out and yours isn't among it. Then, HOORAY. There it is. Drag it off. Put it on the trolley. Then comes the most difficult decision of the holiday. The red or the green channel.

You know you've brought back more than £32 worth of goodies. You've split up your eight bottles of wine and 2,000 fags among your friends. What the hell, go for the green channel.

Smiling cheerfully you push your trolley nervously into the gaping entrance. Four men and a woman eye you up and down. You crash into the person next to you... You push on, sweating profusely. Past the man with his suitcase open and the Customs officer holding up a pair of underpants... ugh.

Almost there. A tap on your shoulder. You freeze expecting to feel the gun in your neck. You turn slowly. It's the old lady from 23B holding up a carrier bag which has fallen off your trolley. Waves of relief – and out you go.

Why do people always look so guilty going through Customs, even when they're not? Could you spot a villain if you were a Customs officer? Have you any idea of how YOU look when you're going through? Don't you think they KNOW you're over the limit? Of course they do. They don't want the little fish – they want the sharks but the Customs hall is a superb place to see we Brits making utter fools of ourselves.

POSSESSIVE PEOPLE

These are different from 'Under-the-thumbites' because they are not the ones who are suffering. These are the people who are so insecure that they have to check on their partner every five minutes. A possessive person will always need to know where their partner is and what they are doing, 24 hours a day, seven days a week. If their partner goes to lunch without them a.) knowing or b.) knowing who they've gone with then there is a major Spanish inquisition later.

'Where did you go?'
'Who did you go with?'
'Why didn't you tell me you were going?'
'Who else was there?'
'What did you talk about?'
'Who did you sit next to?'

This is usually followed by the possessive person having a tantrum and the poor partner keeping quiet and sulking.

Partners of possessive people are also subject to random checks at work or at play. The 'check-up' phone call to the office comes in...

'Who was that who answered the phone?'
'What do they look like?'
'You weren't at your desk; where were you?'
'What have you been doing, then?'
'What time are you coming home?'

They are also likely to be frisked when they walk in. Sniffed for traces of aftershave or perfume. Having their diary checked frequently. Have their pockets and briefcase checked daily. Debriefed on the day's events, and given the once over for not checking in at 3pm.

Possessive people are also likely to think that their partners are having an affair, whether they are or not. They imagine worst-case scenarios constantly and develop worry lines at an early age.

Easy to spot and identify firmly, a possessive person will ALWAYS deny being possessive, even in the face of hard evidence, and their partner will suffer considerable grief later.

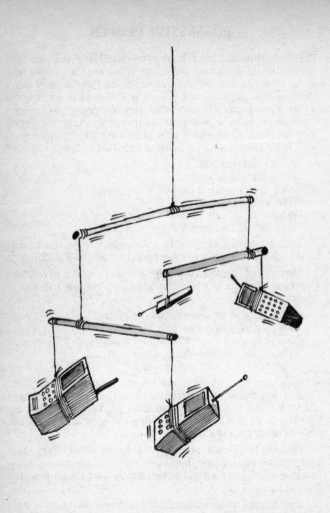

MOBILE PHONES

This was an invention waiting to happen. From the days of Star Trek, someone, somewhere was going to invent a mobile phone. First, it was two cans and a piece of string. It worked but it was slightly impracticable on the M1. Next came Pushbuttons A and B. For this you needed to find a phonebox. Plenty around, but not mobile. Next came Pushbutton phones *per se*. In cute glass surrounds. They were satisfactory and even more plentiful when you could find one which worked. Then came cardphones. Good idea. The trouble with these is that you always have the wrong card or no card at all. So mobile phones were the way to go.

Initial jobs were fitted in Rolls Royces and were very exclusive. Calls didn't get cut off. It all worked well but you needed to be Elton John to afford one. So cellular phones were developed and that's where we are today.

Mobile phones work by radio. They latch on to a 'cell'. The trouble with these phones is that about two million people also latch on to your cell and you are cut off. That's if you can ever find a cell near you to get a decent signal. You get a scratchy conversation, often one way, which terminates just as you get to an interesting bit. For this you are charged £10,000 a second and £25 a month for the privilege of being done. Plus an initial £60 fee 'cos the operators are poor. You have to agree to keep the phone only for five family generations.

The users are the best, though. In comes the PW angle again. The ultimate posing tool, they ring on trains, in restaurants, in the car, on street corners, anywhere. People strike up 'phone poses' when it rings and pretend to be mega-important. In the car they juggle with the phone while negotiating a contraflow, looking very serious indeed.

Some people even arrange for phones to ring just to impress friends. Some have two phones – 'Hold on a mo, I'm on the other line'. The transportables are even funnier. People stagger round with those huge unwieldy things 'because the batteries last longer you know and it's a Class 2 phone'. They look incredibly stupid as it rings in the street and they're left juggling with all the bits.

There is also an unwritten rule with mobile phones. They never work when you need them most. Observe.

PEOPLE IN HOSPITALS

It's a very strange feeling when you go into hospital. Assuming you're not being rushed in for a critical operation, that is. You wander in through the front door and register with reception. From that moment you are tagged. Your name is attached to your wrist. You find your allotted bed and lie on it just to get the feel of it. You feel fine. Why are you here? Then you remember the lump/bump, so you feel a bit queezy. Then you look around you.

Six beds to your portion of the ward. A person in the next bed has the screens around them. Must be about to kick it. Opposite you, a person flat on their back. Not moving. Not good. A wheezing noise from the far bed, followed by anguished coughing. It's now that you begin to feel as if you're in a hospital.

From somewhere down the corridor comes a shriek. Followed by shouting and a smashing of things on the floor. Then the nurse comes in to see you.

'Hello. You must be such-and-such. Welcome to the General Hospital. We hope you'll survive your operation and we look forward to seeing you again soon. Enjoy your stay. Now would you mind please having a quick bath and putting this on'. Hands you a white sheet. Then it all begins.

Next time you're visiting or you're in to have something removed, record some of the happenings around you. The people. The smell. The noise. The decor. How people panic and worry over nothing. How the three words 'This won't hurt' take on new meaning. How macho types suddenly turn to cringeing wimps and how the ugliest nurses and doctors can suddenly become stunners, and the lengths to which people go to try to curry favours from other people.

HAIRY PEOPLE

It isn't their fault, of course. Whoever hands out the hair when we're born presumably has a drink from time to time like the rest of us and gets a little smashed occasionally. Fair chance, then, that one in a hundred of our species will have a surplus of hair on their body. Or no hair at all.

It's the hairy people we're looking at here. Walking Axminsters. Some people like it, some don't. Real he-men in films always have a rug on their chest – look at Burt Reynolds and he hasn't done too badly out of it. It's when the rug appears out of place that the problems start.

People, for some peculiar reason, still have sideburns or sideboards. I'm sorry, but women just don't look like women with them. Others have forearms like an ape. This may keep you warm in winter but it looks positively awful on the beach.

Men are hairier than women. Fact. For some reason hair is not acceptable on women in the Western World and consequently women have to endure weekly agonies getting rid of it. Armpits are mowed regularly, legs are waxed, mowed or Immac-ed. Or all three. Bikini lines are tailored to suit but some women buck the trend. It is not uncommon to see a woman with a moustache. Why she feels this looks good only she knows but you certainly see them.

Men get bored with the whole thing. They let their faces sprout. David Bellamy is a good example. Some men have Axminsters on their back and their shoulders as well as their legs and arms. In fact they have hair everywhere.

One wonders what people would look like with the roles reversed. Plucked eyebrows on men. Beards on women. Waxed legs for men. Hairy chests for women. Shaved armpits for men. Bushy eyebrows for women, and so on. Perhaps one day we'll all wake up to find it's happened.

SIXTY-NINE

Soixante-Neuf. Giggle Giggle. Titter Titter. No other number out of all of them provokes such a reaction in people. Say it at any party and someone will give you a knowing look. It is the ultimate numerical double entendre. Sixty-eight has no effect. Neither does seventy. Sixty-nine does.

You may be wondering why. This book does not propose to go into the finer details as it's a family book but suffice to say that when you write the numbers sideways they resemble one of a number of positions in which some people like to get intimate.

Mathematics has nothing to do with it. Being quiet and shy does. It's normally those quiet people who indulge. The people who titter and shout the loudest about it, pretending to have 'been there and done it all' usually haven't the slightest experience of any such thing.

Try it for yourself when you're out. In the middle of a conversation when you're talking, find an excuse to say, quite innocently, the number sixty-nine and watch for the reactions. If you come from a sheltered background and this is all news to you, you'll have to make your own investigations as to how and why this works, but it does.

For immediate proof, try it in a rugby club.

BEING INTRODUCED TO SOMEONE
YOU KNOW BUT CAN'T REMEMBER

This must be one of THE most embarrassing things that can ever happen to a person. It can happen at work. It can happen socially. It can happen virtually anywhere, at any time. You're standing talking to a group of people when someone you recognise walks over and says hello to you by name in front of everyone. You're about to say hello back when, horror or horrors, you can't remember their name. What do you do?

You can hardly call them 'thing' or 'er', can you? You have only a finite time to get yourself out of the hole before they come out with that crushing line 'You don't remember me, do you?' This is normally delivered after you've gone to great lengths to impress on everyone else what good friends you both were.

So you hope someone else knows them and drops their name into the conversation while you're talking. If not, you're sunk. It's even more embarrassing in a one-to-one situation as you've no get-out and they'll pick up any hesitation straight away. In a business situation it can be vital points lost.

Equally embarrassing is calling somebody the WRONG name throughout a conversation. Most people will correct you once when you do it; after that they won't bother. It's then excruciating when someone tugs your sleeve afterwards and tells you what their REAL name is. By then it's too late.

If it's a semi-amusing thing on which to look back it's even more amusing when you're watching from the sidelines. You see one person becoming more and more put out in the first instance and the other struggling more and more opposite them. In the second instance you can see the former becoming really annoyed but the other person can't see it. It also works well as a set up.

PEOPLE WITH B.O.

You have to be honest and admit that B.O. is not the problem it once was. There was a time, probably before you and I were alive, that no self-respecting man would be seen to go into the bathroom and spray himself with deodorant. Women? Yes. Because in Western civilisations women do not smell. Men just washed regularly and any other smells were deemed to be manly. Things have changed, though, for the better.

Not so in other parts of the world. Even today, for example, there are bizarre rituals in some places where a man, to prove his love for his chosen woman, has to perform certain acts. Those acts have to be carried out when the woman has not washed for a period of two months.

We are, however, far more sophisticated today. Men and women use deodorants and perfumes and 90% of the population wouldn't even dream of going out in public if they emitted an odour. Some people may 'perfume' to excess but that's another problem.

That still leaves 10% and do they stand out, or what? The trouble is, like other PW scenarios, no-one ever does anything about it. Nobody says anything; they just tolerate it and it's fascinating to watch how people moan behind others' backs and just smile sweetly to their faces.

It's not the kind of thing about which you can drop a broad hint, such as leaving a can of deodorant around. The person probably doesn't even realise. Otherwise, they'd do something about it. Some people just have a problem.

The interesting thing when you're watching is that people don't even keep their distance from a 'smelly'. All they do it pull faces to someone else behind the person's back. It's amazing they never get caught.

NAME-DROPPERS

One of the first symptoms of a person losing that line between fact and fiction, namedroppers are everywhere. It's a very definite line and namedroppers clearly tend to fall either side of it.

There are the namedroppers who feel a little inadequate because they don't know many people, have a boring circle of friends, and seek merely to impress people. They are on the side of 'fact'. They know they don't know the people whose names they drop; they're just trying to win admiration by making it appear they do.

The other namedroppers are totally different. They crave stardom. They want to be a star. So they start to invent things in their minds and, when they namedrop, over a period of time – convince themselves that they really have met those people. Again, it's done to impress and for general admiration but in this instance it's not to win friends; it's to gain support for their own 'increasing star status'.

See if you can't spot the difference between the two. People who bump into celebrities as part of their daily life are normally very matter-of-fact about it. Celebrities generally are a boring crowd – it's their exploits which are hyped up – and as such people who mingle with them don't really mention them too much. Namedroppers tend to be excited about the lowliest of names and if they were ever to meet a TV soap 'star' they'd probably have a heart attack at the excitement.

Wicked social crowds sometimes set up namedroppers with fictitious events and meetings and if a namedropper is ever gullible enough to fall for it, it usually cures them for good. They're so embarrassed by it all when they realise.

MAY 29 AND OCTOBER 17

You won't find those dates printed in any diary. You won't find them printed on any calendar. You won't find them recognised in any newspaper. So what are they? They are the 'crossover' days for women.

From mid-April until May 29 in any given year, most women face a crisis decision. Do they, or do they not, opt to venture out of the house without wearing stockings or tights? Too early and they run the risk of being seen with appallingly white legs and blemishes all over them. Too late and they stand out in a crowd.

It's not possible to get your legs brown before April/May unless you own a sunbed machine, so most people do it discreetly out of sight of the neighbours in the garden. More 'Spam-leg'-like specimens throw caution to the wind and venture to the supermarket with nothing on. As May proceeds the decision gets nearer. Do you risk going out or to work with nothing on? If you decide too soon the worst that can happen is that people will think you're a tart. Especially if you wear an ankle chain; and, let's fact it, white legs look daft.

Research has show that May 29 is the average day when most women opt for without. In October, the reverse problem arises. Days are gloomier, the weather gets worse. Do you hang on without hosiery hoping there's enough of your sun tan left to convince everyone else, or do you go back to the top drawer again? The decision gets more and more difficult until October 17 when, again, research shows that most women opt back for their coverings.

So the PW aspect. Spot those who get it wrong.

INSECTS

Insects are a pain in the backside. People like David Bellamy tell us constantly how useful they are but to most of us they're a constant annoyance. They get in your breakfast just as you're about to put a forkful in your mouth. They get in your cup of tea. They swim in the loo, making you think twice before you sit down. Without exception, they make such an irritating noise that moving to the central reservation of a motorway would sometimes be preferable.

Ants are indestructible. Just when you've killed 10,000, along march another three for a night out. Crane flies are suicidal. They just float about asking to be zapped. Wasps are just pure evil.

Whoever invented the wasp had a bad day. No other insect looks as evil or as nasty as a wasp. From any angle a wasp looks mean. Armed with a Scud-like stinger, it bristles with evil as it hovers around. Simply looking at it makes it angry and everywhere you try to move it follows you. Ducking and diving has no effect – it homes in on you looking for the most sensitive place to attack if you give it a good enough reason. They are resistant to most forms of attack. Well-aimed slippers invariably miss. Fly sprays are too weak. Vapona strips they eat. They're far too clever to be fooled by a mauve light in an electric zapper. No. One day wasps will take over the world. They're just waiting for a good excuse.

Flies get everywhere. Like other insects they provide fascinating PW. Watch as people try to smash them into oblivion. See objects go flying. Hear curses such as you've never heard before. Feel a person's anger as the insect beats the odds and lives. Sense the relief when the insect either dies or makes it out of the window.

Also, marvel at how a tiny being often not more than a quarter of an inch across can anger a being 100,000 times its size and often live to tell the tale.

PERSONAL NUMBER PLATES

You may or may not know you can buy your own car registration number. Either by buying a car with it already on and transferring it to your car or by buying a number through a transfer agency. It costs £80 for the transfer fee which goes to the DVLC and someone's new house but the costs of the numbers vary enormously. From £100 to £100,000.

So who buys them? One kind of buyer is the 'I want people to think I've got a new car' type. Obviously, the letter on a number plate generally gives away the year it was bought, so a personalised number makes an older car appear newer. At least, unless the onlooker really knows that make of car they can't work it out from the number plate. Those types of buyers tend to go for the cheaper numbers; four figures and two letters would cost about £1,000. Three figures and three letters would cost more, depending on what the letters and numbers are.

The next kind of buyer is the poser. The 'I want my initials on my car' type. Those kinds of people tend to have their briefcases, wallets, shirts, suitcases and everything else they own monogrammed with their initials. They try to get their two or three letters plus the lowest number possible, preferably ABC 1 but that is extremely expensive, because everybody wants to be No. 1.

The third kind of buyer is the stinking rich. Money is no object. They are the ones who can afford the 'cute' number plates which spell names, jokey words or whatever. Serious money is splashed around, as they are 'one-offs'. It's something to try to spot when you're in a 30-mile traffic jam on a bank holiday.

Finally, there's the fourth and newest breed of buyer. Never slow to miss a bit of dosh, the DVLC has brought in the 'junior' personalised number plate. They are for people who would like a plate but can't afford one yet. Status is a big market nowadays. So they sell, relatively cheaply, new registration numbers when you buy a new car. You still get the year letter at the front but you can have one, two or three numbers plus three letters which can obviously be your initials. People who own them are then marked as serious 'wannabees' who crave status but haven't yet 'made it'. Still, it enlivens motorway driving.

HOW YOUR PARTNER TELLS YOU IT'S TIME TO GO

Not in the sense of 'you're history'. Rather, when you're at a function with a group of people and he or she feels it's time to make a move. There's the 'try to catch your eye over the table' method. This normally makes you ask them out loud if they're OK because it looks as if they've developed a nervous twitch.

There's the 'exaggerated falling asleep' method, whereby your partner nearly ends up with their head on the table. Usually you fail to notice.

There's the 'kick under the table' method. That makes you think you've done something wrong.

There's the continual 'looking at the watch and constantly saying the time' method. What normally happens here is that the host offers more drinks all round, meaning that your partner goes back to square one.

There's the 'contrived excuse' method. Sometimes this works if the excuse has been planned beforehand. It is more likely that you haven't a clue what your partner is going on about and they end up looking very silly.

Then there's the sudden 'illness' trick. One minute your partner is fine; the next minute they're writhing about in agony. A little dramatic, this, but it works.

You may recognise some or all of these scenarios. You may use some yourself but do you really think other people don't know what you're doing?

UFOs

Have you ever seen a UFO? No. Neither have I but there are many people who claim they have. That leaves us to draw one of two conclusions:

i.) They've seen a UFO

ii.) They're telling porky pies.

Now, dismissing those in (ii) as either weirdos, fantasists or just plain extra-terrestrial namedroppers, we can concentrate on those in (i). If they've seen a UFO there must have been someone in it. So we're now into extra-terrestrial PW. What would UFO drivers look like? The perennial image is that of a one-eyed, large-headed, small-bodied figure clad in a 'not of this planet' silver suit but do you think an alien would be that obvious?

If an alien was clever enough to design and build a spacecraft to travel from the planet Zeouniner to here, do you not think they'd try to disguise themselves a little? A clever person would surely realise that walking around on a strange planet looking a bit 'different' might attract attention. It might even attract dissection by the odd scientist or two. Surely, a visiting alien would try to look like that planet's inhabitants, so they wouldn't get their teeth kicked in?

You see the point? Given that people have seen UFOs and that they must have had pilots, they must be among us even now or they'd have been spotted. I don't recall Wogan interviewing an alien in recent years, so it's a fair bet that they haven't been here.

So keep your eyes open. ANYONE around you could be an alien in disguise. Gathering information. Stealing products. Mentally filing things away. They may even have X-ray vision. So, if you suspect someone you know of being an alien, make sure you put on clean underwear every day and write to your MP about them.

BEDROOMS

Most people sleep in a bed. Some people have strange 'torture chamber'-like machines to sleep in like a bath but they have bad backs and we should have some sympathy for them.

Beds live in bedrooms. That's obvious really but we're not talking about beds. We're talking about the room and how it's furnished.

Picture a Saturday afternoon at a football ground. An aggro fan has just consumed his 12th lager of the day and is looking for someone to kick to pieces. A hardnut. A macho man. People quake when they see him but to what sort of bedroom does he go home. As, at some point, he surely must?

Does he go home to a mauve and blue bedroom as befits his team? Probably not. Does he go home to a macho Ferrari Red colour scheme? Again. Probably not. What he probably goes home to is a peach-coloured bedroom with pretty borders and cute lampshades in it. Especially if he has a wife or girlfriend.

Surprised? Don't be, 90% of bedrooms are either designed or furnished by women and men are content to let them do so. The top five colours for bedrooms are:

1.) Peach
2.) Fawn
3.) Pink
4.) Pale Blue
5.) Green

The average double bedroom will also house two lamps, two chests of drawers, one dressing table and four ornaments or pictures.

This is a good one to try at work. Pick anyone and see if you can picture what their bedroom looks like. You'll probably never get to see it but if you ask them, you'll be amazed at how far out you are.

PEOPLE WHEN THEY'RE DRUNK

It happens to us all at some time or other. Some more often than others. Each of us needs our own personal level of alcohol to send us 'over the edge' and each of us reacts in a certain way when we go 'over-the-edge'.

It starts with good intentions. You have a few drinks and you know exactly when you plan to stop but as the evening proceeds you have another, then another. You're having a good time; why stop now? You get to that stage where you feel really good — drink gives you a little more courage and you're on form. A great night but you're well aware that you've had a skinful. Then, one drink pushes you too far and you're gone.

People sometimes are sick. That's the most common symptom when drunk. Your body tries to reject the massive alcohol input.

People get violent. That's the 'not-nice' side of what can then be a fairly hard time for all concerned.

People get giggly. This can be hilarious if a normally quiet person suddenly has fits of the giggles.

People get tired and fall asleep on you. Enough said.

People become brave and do things they might not otherwise do. Sometimes with many regrets.

People become 'loud' with opinions on everything and everyone. What happens then largely depends on who's around at the time.

Whatever, when drunk, the one thing ALL behavioural aspects have in common is that you generally need other people around you to help. Usually, help they do and everyone talks about it for weeks afterwards.

THE MOODY PERSON

One in every four people is officially a moody person. A moody person is someone who, if they don't like a given situation they're in, sulks and lets everyone else know that they're sulking.

A moody person goes into a mood to attract sympathy. Their partner is at the bar talking to someone else and they get jealous. They don't like it. So they go into a mood hoping someone will go to them, as eventually they will, and say 'Is anything the matter?' That gives them the chance to be dramatic and wail about everything and anything, usually bringing up loads of historical 'relevant' instances to add support to the current one as well.

Once someone becomes a moody person it's virtually impossible to change them. It can be minimalised once a person realises that it's not doing them any good. Often it starts because they've been spoilt as a child and they're used to having everything they want. When they can't get it, they become moody. Moodiness gets progressively worse as well.

Although a moody person doesn't realise it, they're often labelled by their friends as just that. As friends become hardened to it and less tolerant of repeated outbursts, the amateur dramatics start to creep in to get the mood to have the same effect. 'Loud' behaviour accompanies the mood. 'Illness'. Lies. Deceit. Wild gesticulations and accusations. Tears. Stamping of feet.

In a relationship it can be terminal. Ask anyone who's been out with someone who's moody for any period of time and they'll tell you that it gradually wears them down to the point where they have to split. They'll tolerate it for a time but then they have to call it a day.

Perhaps you know someone who's moody. What stage have they reached?

PEOPLE WHO DON'T KNOW
WHAT THEY'RE TALKING ABOUT

These you can find anywhere in all walks of life. Sometimes they get away with it. Sometimes they don't. Take food, for example. How many times have you met someone who seems to know everything there is to know about food? Where certain dishes come from. How it's cooked. How it's served; and how, when someone asks a certain question, it becomes obvious that they're a complete fraud.

Wine is another favourite. A great deal of rubbish is talked about wines. Some people – very few – can tell the difference between one bottle of wine and another. Which year. Which region and so on but it's a skill which takes years to perfect. How many times have you met someone who knows EVERYTHING about wines? There's always someone in any group who'll grab the wine list and immediately become 'knowledgeable'.

Ah, yes. You'll like this one; 1986 was a brilliant year for this type of wine and it's not too expensive. Try it. You'll like it. Normally you do but why shouldn't you? No self-respecting restaurant will serve rubbish. It's when that same 'expert' trips up on something obvious that it shows them up. Like when a red is white and vice versa.

Cars are another favourite. A car is a car, right? It gets you from A to B, right? Wrong. In this field there are a million and one experts who know all about classic cars, new cars, future cars, YOUR car and so on – right down to the last nut and bolt. Or at least they pretend they do. They're normally the ones who can't even change a tyre.

Look around you. There's an expert on everything who usually hasn't got a clue what they're talking about.

MISFORTUNES

Elsewhere in this book PW has covered similar situations but it's worth dwelling on how we as humans derive 'pleasure' from other people's misfortunes. Take the situation of someone walking down the road. They're not looking where they're going. SMACK. They walk into a lamp-post or something. What's your first reaction? Do you feel horror? Shock? Sadness? Pain? Or do you laugh? You KNOW what you'd do, don't you?

Someone running for a bus dragging two children and a load of shopping. They nearly make it but the bus drives off. Again, you afford yourself a silent chuckle.

Someone walking under a ladder and something splashing on them or falling on them. Do you rush to help them or do you blame them as it's their fault for doing it?

Someone getting splashed by a passing car in the rain.

Someone tripping in the street.

Someone getting a parking ticket.

Someone having their car clamped or towed away.

Someone who spills coffee down them.

Someone who falls downs the stairs.

As long as it's immediately obvious to us that the person is not badly hurt, our immediate reaction is not one of sympathy. We tend to laugh. Either outwardly or inwardly. We might regret it later but we do it nevertheless.

Keep your eyes peeled. Notice how other people do this or even how YOU do it yourself.

ARE THEY OR AREN'T THEY?

Do you remember the old Harmony Hair Spray TV advertisement? Is she or isn't she wearing a hairspray and the many clean and not so clean jokes which followed it? Well, the same double question can be applied to many things, in life and in PW.

Let's take one specific instance. You can think of some more at a later date. In summer, we sometimes have hot weather and when it's hot in the U.K. it's also very sticky. That's because we suffer from high humidity. Sensible people wear as little as possible, as discussed earlier in this book. Some people take it to the logical fullest extent and leave off EVERYTHING they feel they don't need to wear, i.e., their underwear.

No-one should ever know. It's a big secret only they know. Sometimes they'll divulge this secret over the phone to their loved one as a way or 'warming 'em up' for the evening...

Why do we wear underwear? Self-confidence. Practicality. Convention. Hygiene. All those reasons. People wear standard stuff, lacy stuff, designer stuff, posy stuff; but because it's UNDERwear it remains private to most people and no-one ever knows what YOU are wearing. This then introduces the slightly kinky and sordid aspects when people try to discover, especially for women.

So it's not a subject you could, or would, push too far or it becomes very voyeuristic but, on a hot day, it's legal and decent to let the mind and the vision wander. Are they or aren't they? You can ask yourself the question and look at whoever you might care.

AIRPORTS

An artificial environment. A city within a city. Therefore such places are subject to different behavioural patterns. There's certainly plenty to keep a PW amused when at any airport in the world.

The single most important object in any airport is the Flight Details board. Watch how people sit glued to a TV screen, board and anything with information on it. They wait for the slightest change in their flight. Nobody else's flight matters. It's their flight that is all-important. An aircraft could crash on the runway but as long as their flight was not affected it would be satisfactory.

Airport lounges are awful places. Bodies sprawl everywhere. Flat out, curled up, books over faces, propped against walls. Awful. Especially when flights are delayed. Airport loos are equally awful. They always have the obligatory rivers in them and paper and debris everywhere.

The Duty Free Shop. You find people examining every square inch for 'the bargain of the year', convinced that they're saving a fortune. They might not need half the stuff they buy but what the heck – it's so cheap.

The Bookshop. You can tell a great deal about a person by what reading material they buy for a flight. Note how some people agonise for ages over which book to buy. Note how some people virtually read a magazine before putting it back without paying. Notice how the hypochondriacs stock up with virtually every tablet available.

The cafeteria. Use your own imagination.

Passport control. Why can you never find your passport?

The hand-luggage check. How people moan when they're stopped for a random search. They wouldn't moan so much if they knew someone who'd been blown to pieces by a bomb.

The departure lounge. How people size up each other while waiting for the boarding call. It's probably because you have to spend so much time waiting for an aircraft that you notice so much.

TV SOAPS

If people run their lives by horrorscopes, then TV soaps are a very close number two. The TV soap has replaced the corner shop for gossip and everyday happenings. As the TV has infiltrated our lives more and more, it has become an everyday part of our existence. It goes on at the same times every day and off at the same times – except for special occasions. As such, it's an integral part of most peoples' thinking. The news is real. Sport is real. Current affairs are real.

Soap operas have become real, too. As they're on regularly, they form a part of the daily ritual and people really run their lives around them. Neighbours is immensely popular because of the time it's scheduled. People arrange their whole lunchtime around it and you know they've got it bad when they do it for the same episode in the evening. The characters become an integral part of their lives, too; Joe, Harold, Madge, Caroline – all become familiar names which dovetail very easily into a person's normal life. It's not uncommon to hear people discussing Neighbours in a pub as if they were discussing mutual friends.

It's a very weird facet of everyday life and an addiction in the truest sense of the word. The fact that a TV programme can make someone alter their life around it so as not to miss it is a trifle worrying. It also shows how powerful such a programme can be. Messages can be portrayed. Morals can be influenced. Peoples' minds can be influenced on any subject the producers care to tackle.

Neighbours is generally reckoned to be a family show dealing with lightweight topics. Not so Eastenders, which is far harder-hitting. Do TV soaps affect people? Have you ever spotted clear symptoms of it? Have you noticed people planning their lives around them? Food for thought, eh?

GIFTS

A gift is an exceptional gesture. A card shows that a person is in your thoughts. A gift shows that you've gone out of the way to find a 'small something' for them. The old saying is that 'it's the thought that counts'. What the gift is should become largely irrelevant – but does it?

Weddings take it to extremes. Most people nowadays issue a wedding book, in effect an order book for what they'd like. Not content with receiving a 'gift' as a sign of good wishes, they issue a book which gives the invited guest a choice of what to buy and, thoughtfully, a guide price. They might as well issue an invoice book with it to claim back the VAT. A far cry from a surprise gift.

At Christmas and for birthdays it is sometimes comical. Relatives not wishing to cause offence often ask what the person would like, in effect soliciting an order. The resultant gift is then scarcely a surprise, although most people feign such when they receive it.

Spot, if you will, the flash of ingratitude on people's faces when they don't receive the gift they were expecting. Most people recover quickly and remember their manners but some are rude and go into a sulk – really not what receiving a gift is all about.

Finally, spot how many people leave the price tag on whatever gift it is that they buy. Would you believe that some people do it deliberately so that the other person can see EXACTLY how much money they've spent on them. So that when they receive a reciprocal gift on their birthday they know that they haven't 'lost out'. Scrooge would turn in his grave.

KEEPING UP WITH THE 'JONESES'

You might think this is something which happens only on TV but you'd be wrong. Keeping up with the Joneses doesn't necessarily mean keeping up with your next door neighbour. Nowadays, people living in neighbouring houses aren't usually on the same income and therefore 'keeping up' is scarcely relevant if you can't afford it. If you don't get on with your neighbour, at least you tolerate them. In today's crime-threatened society it would be daft not to do so. You can see obvious instances of neighbours trying to outdo each other but it's rarer than it was.

It's normally in your own social circle that this happens now. You choose your friends because you're compatible, both socially and financially. So it's easier to keep up with them. People do. Sometimes obviously, sometimes not so obviously.

You get something new for your garden and they spot it next time they're round. Next time you go round, they have one, too. A new car? Strange how it spurs them to think about the same thing.

Nobody likes to feel left behind in life and certainly not with friends. Is there anything wrong in trying to keep up? It marks you out as slightly insecure if it gets to a serious level and if it goes too far it can lead to huge rows and eventual falling out of previously happy friends. True friends don't give a damn what you have so long as you, and they, are happy.

QUEUES

A British way of life. In the bible there is a piece which says 'Wherever two or three people are gathered together in my name, then that is a church'. Or something like that anyway. In Britain, wherever two or three people are gathered together then someone will go and join it to form a queue. We queue for everything.

In post offices it's rare not to find a queue. Normally people are content to stand and wait, however long it takes. They enjoy a good gossip. In supermarkets it exhausts your patience but still we do it. You wait ages when someone unloads three trolley loads of food and then they get out the cheque book. Not a whisper. People stand and fume silently.

In banks the queue goes out of the door and down the street. That doesn't stop people queueing. No – they'll join it for the fun of it. Even if it's only a polite enquiry.

In petrol stations people queue patiently for petrol. They'd rather queue than go to another pump a few yards away. On motorways we queue – and how. Stretched back for miles. No fuss. No riots. We just fume in our cars and go back and do it again next day.

Why do people tolerate queues? Why don't people do something about it? They'll stand and moan to the person next to them but they NEVER take any action with people who matter. Everywhere you look, in any town, you'll always see Brits queueing for something.

TERRITORIAL BEHAVIOUR

We all know animals are territorial. Cats are a good example. They won't go off their patch and woe betide another coming on theirs. But did you realise that humans are territorial, too? Football fans are a good example. Anyone goes on their patch from another club and they're dead. If they go to another club they can expect reciprocal action.

Offices are great places to spot people protecting their territory. When someone new joins everyone bands together and for a time the new person is on the 'outside' of all that is happening. People are protecting their territory together. People become angry when someone uses their space, their chair, their desk, their equipment, and so on. You find in office situations that people are quick to set up their own territorial boundaries.

In an office, most people usually have their own desk. That's THEIR desk, their territory and no-one likes to find someone sitting at, and using, their desk. Likewise their chair. It may be a normal chair but it's theirs. Then there's the space immediately round the desk. If someone is working and you step inside where they reckon their boundary is, they will challenge you to find why you're on their patch.

As status grows, it becomes more definable. A bigger desk. A bigger chair. An office. A bigger office. A huge office. A whole floor.

Even at home, couples have their own territories which they don't like even their partners to cross. Not so strongly as at an office but they're there all the same. They're just a little more difficult to spot.

CORPORATE

The word for the 90s. The dictionary definition is:

'Forming a body politic or corporation; forming one body of many individuals; of belonging to a body politic'.

In practice, it means a company going to sometimes absurd lengths to establish a corporate identity and individuals who singularly let it dominate their lives.

Most companies have a logo. A corporate identity. That is then put on stationery, public material — anything the public sees but for some companies that is not sufficient.

Staff have to wear a corporate uniform. With little name badges and cute neckties. Some may wear a corporate watch. With corporate cuff-links. All will have corporate diaries. With entries written in by corporate pens.

All staff will answer the phone the same. 'Good afternoon. This is the Hughes Corporation. My name is Melanie. How can I best serve you, my external customer, today?'

Corporate bodies will have regular meetings and meetings about meetings and numerous memos. Corporate coffee will be served to external customers.

At home and socially, the corporate individual never sways from the cause. When the phone rings they assume their business posture, just in case. Social evenings never happen. They're after-business meetings of mutual business contacts. The corporate individual never misses a chance for business. The home mirrors the office. Corporate.

Corporate people never smile much. They do only what their training manuals and business manuals have taught them to do. Nothing happens unless they say so, in the order that they've been trained to do.

Corporate people are very boring.

MEAN PEOPLE

A 'mean person' is someone who hates to part with money. A poor person is someone who has no money. A rich person is someone who has pots of it. There is a world of difference between the three.

Being involved with a mean person is awful. Every financial transaction is checked and double-checked, often under embarrassing circumstances. You could be in a restaurant with a group of friends. The bill arrives and you agree to divide it between, say, three couples; £40 per couple. Not too bad. Then your partner points out that their starter was cheaper than the others; they drank only one glass of wine compared to everyone else and they didn't have coffee. So please adjust the split. You may think this is trivial but it really is an awful situation to be in.

Restaurants are very good places for glimpsing mean people. They are the ones who are choosing from the menu according to the price, not the dish. Most people eat at restaurants they can afford; a mean person eats at restaurants for the 'pose' value and then proceeds to choose the cheapest dishes. It will always be the cheapest bottle of wine. They will have a dessert only if it's included in the main meal price and they'll have tea or coffee, whichever is cheaper. They will seldom leave a tip, usually finding an excuse to avoid doing so. If they do, it's embarrassingly small.

In a pub they never buy a round. At work they'll never have enough money for a sandwich or coffee. At lunchtime, they'll conveniently have left their wallet back at work.

Mean people don't look poor. Far from it. They look after themselves. Never flash, never flaunting it, but their bank account has far more noughts in the balance column than most of us are ever likely to see.

CROSSING A BUSY ROAD

Do you remember The Tufty Club? Look Right, Look Left, Look Right again. If all clear, quick march. Then there was the Green Cross code. What there is now I don't know. All of them had one prime purpose – to help you get safely across the road. Getting across any road in the 90s is difficult enough; getting across a busy road is a matter of luck.

If you're fit and mentally active you're normally OK if you check both ways and dash for it. If you have any kind of physical or mental handicap, it's a lottery. Even at pedestrian crossings, with or without traffic lights, it's hazardous but we all have to do it.

In a car it's equally difficult. Do you pull out or don't you? When finally you decide to do it a car comes hurtling round the corner at you at 90mph. Consequently, you really see some sights with people trying to get across roads. There are people who are nervous of the push-button lights. There are lights which don't work. Cars which don't stop when they're red. People getting halfway across when the green man turns to red. They then go into blind panic as six lanes of traffic get ready to mow them down. They have a moment's indecision on whether or not to go back or carry on... the cars are revving up... more panic... so they carry on almost running. Eventually they make it with time to spare but when you're out there in the middle of the road you can never anticipate how much time you have left.

Then there are the sporting types. The ones you see in the distance as you're driving along. At the last minute, they dash out in front of you to see if they can beat you getting across the road. Who among us hasn't had a heart-stopping moment followed by that horrible dry-mouthed feeling when this has happened? Then they simply turn around and smile at you sheepishly.

SPORTS POSERS

They always look the business. They are the ones who bowl into the Leisure Centre looking like a million pounds. The latest Reebok trainers, the most expensive shellsuit, the stopwatch round the neck, the sweatbands round the head and wrists. Off comes the top. Wow! A real Nike Professional two-button polo collar double-stitched tennis shirt. Brilliant. At every event at which they turn up, they're dressed the same. Immaculately.

The trouble is they've never done any sport in their life. They're one of those growing number of people who eat four meals a day, doughnuts, cream cakes, Yorkie bars and so on and still lose weight. So they always look slim. Yet they can't do any sport at all. They merely wear the stuff because it looks good.

You see it a great deal on ski holidays. In the hotel or chalet, they are the ones with all the new equipment. All matching. Even down to the straps, cords and lip salve. At the end of the day they still look exactly the same. Unknown to you, while you're thrashing round the slopes, they're taking it easy with cup after cup of coffee in the nearest mountain restaurant.

In leisure centres, they're totally safe. They pose in receptions, around sophisticated gyms, in sports halls, by tennis courts, and so on. Yet you never see them doing anything. In truth, they're probably the ones the teachers ridiculed in PE lessons at school. This is their way of getting their own back.

PROFESSIONS

How can you tell just by looking at them what someone does for a job? Do their clothes give it away? Does their speech pattern give it away? Their topics of conversation, perhaps. It isn't at all easy. It's surprising that they've never turned it into a TV game show because it would work well.

Teachers. How would you spot a teacher out socially? Would they be prim and proper, sounding extremely educated? Or would they be scruffily dressed and slouched over a bar somehwere with hair looking as if they'd been dragged through a hedge backwards?

Architects. Would they be dressed in the latest gear, with the latest hairstyle, and a Porsche parked outside? Or would they be like an explosion in a paint factory with hair looking as if it had seen better days?

Accountants. Slim, suave and sophisticated, being capable of adding up numbers on the spot up to the tenth decimal place? Or a balding, short, fat little person with a jacket which doesn't meet in the middle?

Advertising and PR people. Red tinted glasses, fashionable clothes, speech peppered with 'Daaahling this and daaaahling that'? Or harassed-looking people, face etched with lines and baggy eyes looking set to fall out of worn sockets? Reeking of cigarette smoke?

Retail store managers/manageresses. Middle-aged, paunchy or pear-shaped. Pointed bifocal glasses. Slow, deliberate speech. Pleasant air? Or young and aggressive. Take it or leave it attitude. Let's have your money, John. Designer hairstyles. No time for anyone?

Or the oldest profession of all. How would you, when out socially, be able to tell if a perfectly respectable, good-looking woman was in fact 'on the game'? She'd scarcely advertise the fact to all and sundry, would she? So how would you know? How could you even begin to tell if she wasn't 'dressed for work'? That's how difficult it is. Even experienced PW can't get it right.

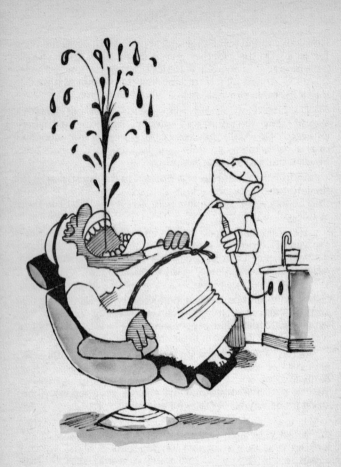

DENTISTS

We looked in detail at surgeons in an earlier chapter. Dentists are similar in most cases but with one or two important exceptions.

(i)   Surgeons like cutting up bodies. Dentists have a fetish for teeth.

(ii)   Surgeons anaesthetise people before they cut them up. Dentists just smile and wade in.

What it takes to become a dentist I don't know but here's an educated guess. Presumably you have to know your way round a mouth without the aid of a map. Neither do you have to mind gazing at the remains of someone's breakfast, dinner and tea all rolled into one. You must not flinch at the spurting of blood from two or three points at once.

You must be strong enough to extract a wisdom tooth with a pair of pliers while standing on a patient's chest. You must be able to design bridges and crowns. You must not shirk from an abcess. You must be able to lie convincingly – this won't hurt.

You must be able to choose the most sensitive spot to begin drilling for oil in a mouth. You must be able to choose an equally sensitive spot to fumble around with that spiky thing. You must be able to strike terror into the heart of your patient with the mere flourish of the needle for an injection.

You must be adept at using gas. You must understand all about X-rays and how to dive for cover when the machine whirrs up. You must be able to use a mouth hoover and make pretty pink drinks which taste horrible. Finally you must not have a conscience as you present your bill to a dazed patient under your 'Dentists Loving Care 12-point plan'.

Sounds a great job. Can't think why I never took it up. What you are doing next week?

SPOTS

Life's little joke. You can guarantee that on the biggest date of your life when you've spent four hours preparing for it, in the most obvious area you'll find a spot; and, just as you're looking at it, it grows to gigantic proportions. Spots are like that.

What makes spots suddenly come, nobody knows. One moment they're not there. The next minute, BANG. There they are. They're generally accepted as being filled with stuff that's 'not nice' and when you pick it once too often, out it comes. Result? An even bigger spot.

Some people are unlucky. They have spots all over from very early on and can never get rid of them. Other people blame the sudden emergence of spots on their diet. It's true. A constant diet of fried breakfast, Big Mac and double chips, Kentucky Fried Chicken, and fish and chips through the day does not help much but how a bit of chicken or fish finds its way into your cheeks is a mystery.

A great deal of money is made out of spot cures. You rub it on and in the morning magically the spot goes. Well, it never really does but it shrinks to an acceptable level so the status quo is resumed. It shows how vain we are to worry about such things. If one of your arms dropped off you might have cause for concern – but a spot? Can you remember having chicken pox? Those are generally reckoned to be the worst type of spots you can get because they get everywhere and they itch like hell. Perhaps we shouldn't eat chickens in any form. They seem to cause plenty of problems.

AEROBICS

A craze which started in the States and never really went away once it arrived here. Various names came from it – Pop Mobility, Dance-fit, Keep Fit to Music and so on but aerobics is what it's all about.

It was supposed to be a fun way of keeping fit. For those who couldn't run three miles a week, walk five miles a week, or cycle 10 miles a week, aerobics was the answer. In village halls up and down the country, weekly classes sprang up. Usually run by Gill, or Lynne, or Sue, or Debbie. For £2 you could buy an hour of jumping about to Michael Jackson and Diana Ross records but that was the start of it. Two years ago very few men did aerobics. More do now. In the formative years, it was the women who made it happen. The £2 may have bought you the dance class but you still had to buy the two-sizes-too-small leotard, the shiny tights, the headband, the thick ankle socks and the expensive trainers to suit. A reasonably big outlay.

In the village hall, it was, and still is, a sight to see. Our class teacher stands at the front of the hall with a tiny portable stereo. Off goes the pause button and horrible loud, distorted music thuds out.

'OK girls, now one, and two, and three, and four and bend those legs and bend those knees'.

The trouble is, most girls in two-sizes-too-small leotards can't bend or they'd split the things. Or do themselves some serious damage. They have to wear two-sizes-too-small or they'd look like beached whales rolling about. After much puffing and panting the hour is over. Little podgy red faces are huddled in corners. Then they all go down to the pub. So any fat tempted away by the exercise returns instantly.

Still, it passes the time and it's sociable. The PW aspect is if you ever get to see a session it's a sight you won't forget for a long time.

WHEN YOU FANCY SOMEONE –
THE BRUSH TECHNIQUE

You've had your eye on them for ages. You fancy them like mad. A chat-up line is out of the question because they know you too well and it would sound corny. You haven't the courage to play footsy and, even if you had, you can't engineer a situation to get half a chance. So what do you do? Get someone to say 'Here, my mate fancies you?' Of course you don't. It has to be far more subtle.

You need to make them notice you without the fear of embarrassment on either side. Here are two scenarios.

i.) You're out in a pub – again. The person you fancy is standing talking to a group of friends between you and the loo. Here's your chance. You set off to the loo, routeing yourself via your intended. As you pass, brush your hand or arm against them. It's a casual enough thing to do but it will cause them to turn and look at you. In that moment you'll know instinctively whether you're in with a chance or not by their response. In one moment you have physical contact and eye contact. Both will give you your answer and if it's negative neither party is embarrassed, as they can choose to ignore it if they wish. If it's positive they will reciprocate in some fashion.

ii.) Much the same technique. When someone you like passes you something like a drink, money, a book, or whatever, you have the same chance. A casual brush of the hand, a stroke as you receive the object, a moment's hesitation. That will once again give you the eye contact which says it all. A positive reaction will bring a long eye contact; a negative one will bring an aversion of the eyes. Either way, you get your answer.

It all sounds a little desperate and pre-planned but it's not. It's very natural but pointed out like this it just sounds odd.

COMPUTER WIZARDS

It's not really a profession. It's not really an occupation but some people are genuinely turned on by computers. They forsake partners in real life to spend more time with their machine.

You might think this is something out of a science fiction film but it's not; it's true. It's an obsession which starts at school age. The fascination that a machine can do things that they can't and provide access to things that normally wouldn't be available.

Computer wizards have highly analytical minds. They might appear unremarkable in normal life but, in front of a computer, they're dynamite. Some have developed remarkable programs which have made everyone's lives easier. Ten years ago word processors didn't exist. Someone, somewhere, dreamed up the first program and look what followed.

You don't normally find computer wizards in offices. You don't find them in factories. You find them in amusement arcades. They are the people who can score five million on a games machine with their eyes shut when you can manage only 43. They're also good at mending little things which normally fox most of us.

The sad thing is that these people are normally lonely and they turn to their computers for comfort. As they spend so much time with their machine, it becomes their comfort, friend and confidante. They never seem to earn much money for originating brilliant programs; the company does which markets them. So if you spot a computer wizard, be pleasant to them. They're an unloved breed.

HOW TO TELL WHEN SOMEONE
IS LYING

It's supposed to be easy. But unless you really know what to look for, it's anything but. You could invest in a lie detector but that is a little drastic. It's best to combine a few tell-tale signs and judge for yourself. Skilful people watching at its best and put to good use. That's why it's the last thing in the book.

Eye aversion. A person who's lying can never look you in the eye properly. Some people can, with practice, but if it's a major lie they will look anywhere but straight at you. Usually at the floor or at something behind you.

Straight expression. Normally, someone who's lying will be trying very hard to control their facial expressions. In a normal situation, a person's face will convey emotion and support to what they are saying. A lying person will have a 'straight' face as they are fighting to suppress any guilty signals.

Flushing. Because they are trying so hard for self control in a stressful situation, a person lying will normally flush slightly if they feel their case weakening in any way. Even if you can't prove that they're lying, confronting them with a hunch may bring a guilty reaction.

More rapid breathing. A sign of stress.

Twitching and fiddling. Again, more signs of stress. These are more obvious if the person is sitting down because they've nothing else to do with their limbs.

Sweating. A person under stress will perspire more freely.

None of these symptoms on their own is enough. You need a combination to be sure. Even so, you'd never convince a jury with it.

END OF PART ONE

You now have 100 scenarios to observe at your leisure. By doing so, it'll give you ideas for 100 more. As you can see, there's really nothing to it but observing what goes on around you.

People Watching has helped people in business, in sport, in health, and in life generally. It allows you to gauge other people before they're aware you're doing so. Sometimes, this can give you an advantage.

It's taught on some training courses and crosses over into Body Language. This is a very similar area, as it trains you to look for signals given off by other people.

If reading this book has done nothing else, it will have made you more aware of instances around you. Some are blindingly obvious when you sit and read them in print; others you may never have even noticed previously.

Observing what goes on around you can help you get on in life. It DOES give you the upper hand, because the more you do it, the better you become at it. It gives you the ability to second-guess what someone is going to do and sometimes even say. In a business environment, that can sometimes be the difference between winning and losing a deal. In a social setting, it provides a good laugh.

Thanks for buying and reading this book. I've thoroughly enjoyed compiling it and, who knows, there may well be another one soon? By which time you'll be on the advanced course.

NEIL TAYLOR

PEOPLE WATCHING T-SHIRT OFFER

You've read the book, now buy the T-Shirt. There are no plans for a film starring Madonna.

Great for holidays, bed, gardening and eventually as a better duster than the one you have now. The design is shown below and is printed in full colour on a top quality white cotton T-shirt. Guaranteed colourfast and shrinkproof; if it does, write to your MP.

Sizes – Small, Medium, Large and Extra Large; simply state clearly which you'd like.

Show the world you're a People Watcher.

Price: £10 each including postage, packing, VAT and a free People Watching sticker.

Please make cheques/POs payable to: CHERUB PROMOTIONS.

FRONT OF T-SHIRT

Mailing address:

People Watching
T-Shirt Offer
PO BOX 100
Whitstable
Kent CT5 3YR

Allow 28 days for delivery.